Searching For The Spirit

Tom Jones

God Bless you

DEACON TOM

HEB 6:19,20

ISBN:10:1548801038
ISBN-13:978-1548801038

PREFACE

While you are reading this book my hope and my prayer is for you to not only begin searching for the Spirit, but also to find the Spirit. Whether you are a Christian or not the Holy Spirit of God can be elusive. Our lives are so packed with things to do and places to go. We are a busy people. I honestly believe if anyone slows down and spends some meaningful time in prayer and scripture reading then your life will be transformed. Your eyes will be opened to a whole new world that is all around you and you didn't even realize it. Are you ready to open your heart and let your life be guided by the will of the Spirit.

CONTENTS

1 Searching For The Spirit

2 Ministry Moments

3 Called To Be A Deacon

4 New Friends Along The Journey

Tom Jones

ACKNOLEDGEMENTS

I would like to give thanks to everyone who purchased my first book, Feelings From the Heart Whispers of the Spirit. Your feedback on how much you enjoyed the book was an inspiration to me and it was affirmation that God had indeed led me to write that book. So many of you have asked me to write another book and after much prayer and consideration I felt God had moved me to write this book.

SPECIAL THANKS

I would like to say thank you to my wife Karen for all of her support. Also, I have had some mentors along the way at just the right time in my life. Two important mentors for me were my basketball coaches John Lenders and Chris Babler. A very special thank you goes to my pastor when I was in high school, Pastor Jack Story.

CHAPTER ONE
SEARCHING FOR THE SPIRIT

Searching For The Spirit

I will go through life and work my plan
Live by instinct and be my own man
Charging ahead come what may
Right or wrong I will do it my way

I am a leader with a strong work ethic
The respect I achieve is somewhat epic
But along the way I begin to ask why
I can't find peace no matter how hard I try

With plenty of knowledge but lacking wisdom
One foot in the world and one in the kingdom
There is no peace serving two masters
Words from the mouths of a couple of pastors

I am successful but there must be more
Is this all the meaning of life has in store
After attending an event as a Promise Keeper
Filled with the Spirit I began to look deeper

Prayer opens my heart and clearly I see
The meaning of life is not about me
Focusing on others and God's desire
Living with purpose and a renewed fire

Lives are changing as I climb this mountain
Blessings are flowing from a spiritual fountain
I am enjoying life as I live my dream
Finally life is peaceful as a mountain stream

The meaning of life I feel I am near it
As I journey in faith "Searching For The Spirit"

When I was a young man I was all wrapped up in this world. My career was what defined me more than anything else. I was raised to have a strong work ethic and it was my responsibility to provide for my family. I worked hard but like everyone else I made a lot of mistakes. But that never slowed me down. Sometimes when Karen and I look back we just laugh at ourselves and some of the things we did. It was like I was charging up a mountain and I would take a shot right between the eyes. I would get up, wipe the blood off and continue charging up the mountain. That is how you live when you lack wisdom. Sooner or later you will stop and wonder what is really important in this life. The impact we have eternally is the most important part of our lives.

In 1994 after attending a Promise Keepers event my life changed. I feel the Holy Spirit spoke to me in a powerful way about the importance of my relationships. My relationship with God, myself, my family and everyone else in my life was my new focus. I felt a fire rekindled deep down inside me and my life took on a new passion. This is when I began searching for the Spirit. As this connection was made on a deep and personal level my restless heart went away and it was replaced with a peace that is hard to explain.

I am more in tune with the Spirit now than at any other time in my life. The result is me being much more aware of other people and the needs they have. Sometimes it can be as simple as just being a good listener as they share what is going on in their life. Other times the Spirit may lead me to do something that really stretches me way out of my comfort zone. This is how I ended up doing mission work in Kenya. I believe our relationships are the most important thing we have to leave an eternal impact on other people's lives. The effects of our relationships will live on long after we pass from this world to the next.

I would like to challenge you to ask yourself this question. What would I want people that I know to write on my tombstone? Do you think they would write what you would like them write? If not, could it be time for you to pause and search for the Spirit? It is never too late to change. Try living a day and not be in a hurry. Stop and talk to people everywhere you go. Call someone on the phone you have not talked to in a while. Better yet go give them a visit and just sit and enjoy each other's company. I would be willing to bet you will have a great day. There is a lot more to life than being busy and keeping a schedule.

One thing in life that I really enjoy is bow hunting for Elk out west with my son. There is just something special about being in the mountains. You become keenly aware of your surroundings and your senses are on high alert all the time. The presence of wolves, black bear, mountain lion and grizzly bear definitely make life a little more interesting. The picture on the cover of this book was taken in the Targhee Mountain range in Idaho.

Over the years I have drawn several comparisons between Elk hunting and the Holy Spirit. Elk are very elusive in the mountains. A successful day is when you have an encounter that gets your heart pounding and you feel an adrenaline rush that makes the hair stand up on the back of your neck. At that moment your life has risen to another level and the feeling is unforgettable. I experience this same feeling when I have an encounter with the Spirit. Cold chills run up and down my spine with my adrenaline pumping and sometimes I can almost feel weightless. It is truly an encounter that is also unforgettable. You never know where the elk are or when you will have that encounter. The same can be said of the Holy Spirit.

John 3:8
⁸ The wind blows wherever it pleases. You hear its sound, but you cannot tell where it comes from or where it is going. So it is with everyone born of the Spirit."

The Holy Spirit is sovereign and he works as he pleases on the renewal of the human heart. You never know which way you will be led or when the encounter will come. Just like the wind the Spirit cannot be seen but the effects of the Spirit can be clearly seen and may be a life changing event.

Targhee Mountains Idaho

When we are hunting in those mountains it is truly a wilderness. Anytime you are in the wilderness there is danger. When we are in this environment we carry items with us that are necessary for our protection. You never know when we may have an encounter with wolves, mountain lions or bears. In our everyday lives the world is a wilderness and we need to equip ourselves with the necessary items for protection. The wilderness I am talking about cannot be seen just like the wind. Spiritual warfare is the fight between good and evil that goes on constantly around us and inside of us. This is why it is essential to search for the Spirit because he will be your comforter and your counselor.

John 14:15-17 [15] **"If you love me, keep my commands.** [16] **And I will ask the Father, and he will give you another advocate to help you and be with you forever—**[17] **the Spirit of truth.**

Ephesians 6:10-18   Finally, be strong in the Lord and in his mighty power. Put on the full armor of God, so that you can take your stand against the devil's schemes. For our struggle is not against flesh and blood, but against the rulers, against the authorities, against the powers of this dark world and against the spiritual forces of evil in the heavenly realms. ...

There are game trails and foot paths all over the Targhee National forest in the mountains. It is easy to navigate as long as you stay on the path. When you venture off the trail and trek deep into the woods a new set of factors enter into your experience. Everything looks the same in the middle of a pine forest. Your path is no longer obvious especially in the dark. When you make a decision to go a certain direction and your decision is wrong, you begin walking farther and farther away from your destination. If you continue on this course for too long then you can become lost. That is why it is necessary to carry a compass or better yet a GPS so you can navigate unfamiliar ground.

It is the same in our Christian journey. Everything seems to fall into place when we stay on the path God has set for us. However, when we veer off the path we become exposed to a world that is full of temptation. Suddenly the direction you should go becomes less clear. It is easy to take a wrong turn and stray from God's will. The longer you stay on this course the farther away from God you become. The Holy Spirit is our moral compass to show us the right way to turn in order to make it back to the path God has set for us.

Matthew 26:41 **41 "Watch and pray so that you will not fall into temptation. The spirit is willing, but the flesh is weak."**

Hunting in the mountains is physically demanding. Often we begin our walk and climb two hours before daybreak. The spot we want to hunt may be three miles away from the vehicle and most of the walk involves climbing the mountain. Your backpack only contains the items that are vital to your trip. Any excess weight only serves to slow you down and becomes a burden for no reason. As we climb our mountain of life sometimes we carry excess baggage. This baggage is not necessary to take with us and only serves to hold you back and slow you down.

In my first book, "Feelings From The Heart, Whispers Of The Spirit", I wrote a poem called "Let It Go" which is about bitterness and guilt. Bitterness over things that have happened or bad things other people have done to you. Guilt about something you have done in your past. Listen to me when I tell you this is excess baggage. Your life is being negatively impacted because of the burden you carry with you and it is simply not necessary. You need to be free from this heavy weight you bare. Whoever, treated you badly in the past forgive them and let it go. If you are feeling guilty about your past, then ask God to forgive you and he will. Let this excess baggage go and free your heart so you can enjoy this life which is a gift from God. You will never experience peace while you carry this load. Please, let it go.

Matthew 11:28-30

[28] "Come to me, all you who are weary and burdened, and I will give you rest. [29] Take my yoke upon you and learn from me, for I am gentle and humble in heart, and you will find rest for your souls. [30] For my yoke is easy and my burden is light."

Imagine yourself sitting on top of a mountain. The sky is blue and there is a gentle wind in your face. As you look out across God's beautiful creation you feel a sense of awe and wonder. Your soul is free and you are filled with joy. You can't stop the smile that is on your face and you thank God for all he has done for you. You almost feel as weightless as the butterfly you watch darting back and forth in front of you. At this moment your heart is as peaceful as it ever gets. This is what it feels like to be filled with the Spirit.

Filled with the Spirit

What is it like to be filled with the Spirit
No other feeling on earth can come near it
Your burden is light and your soul is free
I close my eyes which enables me to see

You cannot predict when it will come
Directly from heaven is where it is from

Tom Jones

Sometimes there is a message to be heard
Other times just the feeling without a word

My body is electrified with chills down my spine
My mind is clear as I wait for a sign
The peace I feel inside is unexplainable
This is the only way this peace is attainable

I don't hear voices only thoughts in my mind
Filled with wisdom and insights I find
A gentle nudge on changes of direction
The changes were needed upon reflection

You ask, how can I feel the Spirit
Ask God in your prayers so you can hear it
Pray and listen as you begin your search
Spend more time with people at your church

Reflect and meditate on your life
Ask God for peace and to clear your strife
Our God loves you with all his heart
Love him back is how you start

Open your heart to receive his word
Don't be afraid to leave the comfort of the herd

Following the Spirit will be a personal journey
Put your faith in God and be free of worry

God will take you places you never dreamed
The old life is gone since you have been redeemed
Boldly accept God's plan and never fear it
This is what is like to be "Filled With The Spirit"

John 14:25-27

[25] **"All this I have spoken while still with you.** [26] **But the counselor, the Holy Spirit, whom the Father will send in my name, will teach you all things and will remind you of everything I have said to you.** [27] **Peace I leave with you; my peace I give you. I do not give to you as the world gives. Do not let your hearts be troubled and do not be afraid.**

I have had Christians ask me how they can get close to the Spirit. They tell me that they have never had a strong spiritual experience that could be attributed to the Holy Spirit. To find the Spirit you don't have to look very far. I would like to share a story with you from a book by Myles Monroe called "The Power Of Vision".

In the mid-twentieth century, in Bangkok, Thailand, the government wanted to build a large highway through a village. Yet in the path of the planned road was a Buddhist monastery with a little chapel, so they had to relocate the monastery-including a heavy, eleven-foot clay statue of Buddha-to another place. Using a crane, the government workers moved the monastery in sections. When the workers transported the statue of Buddha to the new location they began to lower it into place. However, the clay on the statue started to crumble and fall off.

The people were afraid because this was a precious religious symbol to them, and they didn't want it to be destroyed. Yet the more the workers tried to place the statue, the more it fell apart until, eventually, all the clay was falling off. Suddenly, the workers stared in amazement because, as the clay fell away, something unexpected was revealed: The statue was pure gold underneath. Before the statue was moved, people thought it was worth about fifty thousand dollars. Today, that golden Buddha is worth millions and, because of the story behind it, is visited by hundreds of thousands of people every year.

Imagine for a second the gold inside that statue was the Holy Spirit inside of you. Right inside of you is something more precious and valuable than you can imagine. There are scores of people that would love to see the fruits of the Spirit shine from you like the warm rays of the sun on a summer day. You possess your own personal comforter and counselor twenty four seven. But some Christians don't even realize it. Some Christians cover themselves with a protective outer cover similar to the clay on the statue. That covering can take on many different forms. It could be sin in your life that you can't or won't control. Possibly bitterness or guilt that I mentioned earlier is holding you back. Or maybe your protective cover is simply there to define your comfort zone which you won't dare step out of.

I would be willing to bet that some of you reading this right now are restless. You think there should be more to life. You think you could be doing more but you just don't know what. Still others at one time had a dream but now it is a distant memory.

I think this is good illustration of the fact that the Holy Spirit is the gold that dwells inside us. Indeed all we have to do is look inside ourselves to find the Holy Spirit. He is there all the time. Just like the gold the Holy Spirit has a tremendous amount of value. The problem is just like that statue we are covered with clay and the Holy Spirit is not visible. This clay can come in many forms but the results are the same. We form a protective cover around our hearts and our lives so we stay in our comfort zone. This protective cover is a choice we have made. Any choice we make can be changed. Make the choice to let everyone you come in contact with see the gold inside of you which is the Holy Spirit.

What will your legacy be when you leave this world? I believe your relationship with God, your family and everyone you come in contact with is the meaning of life. Your life will change for the better once you take the focus off of yourself and direct it others.

Acts 20:35
In everything I did, I showed you that by this kind of hard work we must help the weak, remembering the words the Lord Jesus himself said: 'It is more blessed to give than to receive.' "

One thing I really love about writing books is slowing down and deeply thinking about life. Spending an abundant amount of time in prayer and meditating on my life and whether I am having the impact I would like to have. Sometimes it is good to reflect back on your life. You have to know where you have been to make the best of where you want to go. We only get one shot at life so let's all try to make sure we are focused on what is really important.

Why are we here? Do we have a purpose? Scientists will tell us, we are just another animal trying to survive in this sometimes harsh world. We have made it to the top of the food chain and that is our claim to fame. Don't you ever believe it because there is so much more to life. We are children of God made in his image. Each of us is unique and our purpose in this life is unique. That makes each of us very valuable as we build God's kingdom.

We show the love of God through our actions and that is how the kingdom of God is built. **John 13:34,35 A new command I give you: Love one another. As I have loved you, so you must love one another. By this all men will know that you are my disciples, if you love one another.**

So how can we show love for one another? One way is to be attentive to the people we encounter every day. As we journey through this life we continually encounter people that are struggling in their journey. If we take the time to really pay attention we can see these people as they cross our path. When we allow our lives to be guided by the Spirit good things happen.

A Divine Appointment

As I journey day by day
I depend on the Spirit to show me the way
Is there someone along the way I need to meet
Maybe someone I see on the street

I pray for God to send someone my way
Perhaps my role is to encourage them today

Tom Jones

I conduct my business while being aware
Someone out there may need me to care

Perhaps a coworker I see every day
Generally we speak with little to say
But today is different for something is wrong
Usually wearing a smile but today it is gone

We all have problems that's for sure
Peace and joy are not always secure
Doing something as simple as lending an ear
Looking deep in their eyes I can see their fear

My heart is heavy as I hear their story
They want to be restored to an earlier glory
I am praying to God as I hear them speak
Let me help them find the peace that they seek

Emotions are building and their ready to explode
Lord give me the words to lighten their load
Right now what they need is someone to care
Listening without judging while their problem
they share

They listen to words that are from my heart
The words are not a cure but they are a start

Needing some encouragement along the way
I simply try to help them through the day

This scene plays out again and again
It may be a stranger or it could be a friend
Was our meeting by chance, I say no way
"A Divine Appointment" is what happened today

If you pray for the Holy Spirit to bring people across your path for a purpose then you will encounter these people. The question is will we be in tune to the guiding of the Spirit to even recognize the opportunity? We as Americans keep a heavier schedule than any other country on the planet. Sometimes I think we are so intent and focused on keeping the schedule that the most important moments in life can get by us.

I have had times in my life where I am thinking back on the day and I realize a certain person that I encountered was showing signs of needing some help. It may be I heard the words they were saying but did not let them sink in deep enough to really pick up on what they were telling me. Or it could have been their body language. Subtle changes like the lack of a smile that is normally there. A sigh while they are speaking or the lack of eye contact. This tells me that they are preoccupied with a deeper matter than the simple conversation we are having. All of these signs are there for us to see but will we take the time to pick up on them?

Let me share a story with you that will illustrate how a simple friendly encounter can turn in to a very significant event. I struck up a conversation with a guy while we were on vacation. I liked the guy right away and was enjoying our conversation. I felt as if there was something pressing on his mind and I asked him, are you alright? He replied no, there were some personal issues that he was dealing with in his life but he did not care to share what the issues were. I told him I would pray for him and he thanked me for the offer. The next day I thought I would give him a copy of my first book, "Feelings From the Heart Whispers of the Spirit". I have had many people tell me they felt the book was encouraging to them. I wanted to give him the book as a goodwill gesture as I thought it might be a source of encouragement for him.

When I gave him the book he shared the issue he was struggling with was being separated from his wife and young daughter. They had separated six months earlier and had not spoken for four months. He told me the marriage was over and the thought of not seeing his daughter was weighing on his heart. I asked him if he believed in God and he said yes. I offered to pray with him and he accepted. It was a short prayer asking God for reconciliation between him and his wife along with the door being open for him to spend time with his young daughter.

The next day I spoke with him again and he told me he had read my book. I was surprised as I said , "you read my book last night" and he said yes he did. He told me the part I wrote about my marriage really stuck in his mind. He was sitting in a chair and looking at the book which was sitting on the table. The more he thought about what he had read the more he thought he had possibly done marriage wrong. At that very instant the phone rang and it was his wife.

I asked him was it a good conversation? He said he started the conversation with telling his wife he thought he had done marriage wrong. The conversation went very well and he was going to call her again after work. A couple days later I saw him again and I asked him if he had another good conversation with his wife. He replied that he had spoken with his wife several times and they were planning to meet on the weekend. He shared his belief they were going to try to get back together.

My heart was filled with joy for this family. Out of curiosity I asked him why his wife had called after four months of no interaction. He said he wondered the same thing so he had asked her why she called in the first place. She said she did not have a reason to call other than she just felt she should. This sent cold chills up and down my spine. I believe in my heart that the feeling to call came directly from the Holy Spirit. Praise God. I still do not know if they got back together or not. All I know is, I was led by the Spirit to pursue this encounter and as a result they were given a second chance to save their marriage.

The Spirit Everlasting

There is a power like no other
Can we take a second and talk my brother
Some say it started back at Pentecost
The disciples gathered after Jesus they lost

A wind from heaven filled the room
All were amazed I would assume
Tongues of fire above each disciple's head
Fear was gone and replaced with power instead

Their ministry consisted of signs and wonders
People everywhere were saved in large numbers
Jesus is the Christ there is no doubt
The signs and wonders were the disciples' clout

So what does this mean for you and me
We have this Holy Spirit don't you see
He acts as a comforter by our side
Also a counselor to be our guide

I have never had tongues of fire above my head
But I know it was for me Jesus died and bled
I feel the Spirit deep down inside me
He gives me joy and a heart that is free

I have had times when my body is electrified
The result is wisdom and feeling satisfied
Some don't believe me but I don't care
Because I know in my heart the Spirit was there

All my problems, fears and doubt on him I am
casting
I receive joy, peace and wisdom from the
"Spirit Everlasting"

Have you felt the power of the Spirit. What a joy that surpasses anything this world has to offer. The Spirit works on us from the inside out. Concepts of peace, joy, happiness, hope, faith and love have their origin inside each of us. Not so coincidently this is where the Holy Spirit abides. All of the things on this earth that are really important come from our hearts.

Have you been searching for something more in your life? Maybe the quality of your life is good. You have been successful but now you are looking for significance. Whatever your reasons may be, you are searching. Let the Spirit take control of your life and begin a new journey. When you allow other people to see the Spirit inside of you they will see love.

1 Corinthians 13:13
And now these three remain: faith, hope and love. But the greatest of these is love.

If you are not a Christian then listen to what I am about to tell you. God loves you more than you will ever know. Jesus Christ is the son of God. We are all born into this world separated from God and all his love. God gave his only son to form a bridge connecting us to him. If you believe Jesus is the son of God and he was crucified on the cross for your sins then you are nearly there. Confess with your mouth that these things are true and three days after his crucifixion, he was raised from the dead then you will be saved. When you are saved you receive the gift of the Holy Spirit.

Romans 3:23 For all have sinned and fall short of the glory of God.
Romans6:23 For the wages of sin is death, but the gift of God is eternal life in Christ Jesus our Lord.
John 3:16 For God so loved the world that he gave his one and only son, that whoever believes in him shall not perish but have everlasting life.
Romans 10:9,10 That if you confess with your mouth, Jesus is Lord, and believe in your heart that God raised him from the dead, you will be

saved. For it is with your heart that you believe and are justified, and it is with your mouth that you confess and are saved.

Everyone that is saved possesses the Spirit with all his power to change your life. As we mature as Christians we will begin to display the fruits of the Spirit.

Fruits of the Spirits

Doing the good of the Spirit within
Is the direct opposite of living in sin
We must put away our deeds of the sinful nature
We receive the Spirit and become a new creature

Never underestimate his passion and desire
For if you do your results could be dire
Those who sow to please their sinful nature
Will reap the destruction of that nature

However those who sow to please the Spirit
Will reap eternal life from that Spirit
The fruits of the Spirit are based in love
Joy, patience, kindness and the peace of a dove

The idea is to care for others more than your self
Putting hatred, rage, and impurity on the shelf

Carry the burden of others as our own
You will be blessed for the love you have shown

Our actions change when the Spirit controls
Helping others through life is one of our goals
The Spirit and God are one in the same
To help us bear fruit is why the Spirit came

There are so many things in life to pursue
The ones you choose are all up to you
When you accept Jesus eternal life you inherit
Peace comes from sharing the
"Fruits of the Spirit"

Galatians 5:16-25
**[16] So I say, walk by the Spirit, and you will not
gratify the desires of the sinful nature. [17] For the
sinful nature desires what is contrary to the Spirit,
and the Spirit what is contrary to the sinful
nature. They are in conflict with each other, so
that you are not to do whatever[a] you want. [18] But
if you are led by the Spirit, you are not under the
law.**
**[19] The acts of the sinful nature are obvious: sexual
immorality, impurity and debauchery; [20] idolatry
and witchcraft; hatred, discord, jealousy, fits of**

rage, selfish ambition, dissensions, factions [21] and envy; drunkenness, orgies, and the like.
[22] But the fruit of the Spirit is love, joy, peace, forbearance, kindness, goodness, faithfulness, [23] gentleness and self-control. Against such things there is no law. [24] Those who belong to Christ Jesus have crucified the sinful nature with its passions and desires.[25] Since we live by the Spirit, let us keep in step with the Spirit.

As Christians our actions speak louder than words. Anyone should be able to look at your life and see that you are a Christian. With these verses in his letter to the Galatians, Paul draws a stark contrast between the actions associated with the sinful nature and the fruits of the Spirit. We are not always successful at fighting the sinful nature but we need to be diligent doing the best we can. None of us have a prayer to be without sin. Jesus was the only one. As we mature we begin to show less signs of the sinful nature and more signs emulating from the fruits of the Spirit.

For me the turning point was when I changed my life focus from me to other people. I started to really focus on my relationships. Your relationships improve when you begin to see those relationships through the other person's eyes. There is no better feeling than sharing the fruits of the Spirit with another person so they can experience joy,

love, kindness, patience or peace. I have found my
greatest peace and joy by helping other people.

Paul talks about this peace he receives from
the Spirit in **Philippians 4:11-13. ¹¹ I am not saying
this because I am in need, for I have learned to be
content whatever the circumstances. ¹² I know
what it is to be in need, and I know what it is to
have plenty. I have learned the secret of being
content in any and every situation, whether well
fed or hungry, whether living in plenty or in
want. ¹³ I can do all this through him who gives me
strength.**

No matter what the circumstances Paul finds
himself in, he is content in the Spirit. This kind of
peace comes from the inside out. I am not saying
he didn't experience emotion. He was happy at
times and sad other times. But, that peace and joy
that comes from the inside cannot be stopped by
external circumstances. For me this special kind of
peace only comes from knowing God and following
the Holy Spirit's guidance. So when you begin
searching for the Spirit one thing you will find is
peace.

Paul also shows us the mindset we would
strive to keep at all times if possible. For our own
good we should not worry and we should control
our thoughts. In his letter to the Philippians he
outlines the mindset that is healthiest for us to
have.

Philippians 4:4-8
[4] Rejoice in the Lord always. I will say it again: Rejoice! [5] Let your gentleness be evident to all. The Lord is near. [6] Do not be anxious about anything, but in every situation, by prayer and petition, with thanksgiving, present your requests to God. [7] And the peace of God, which transcends all understanding, will guard your hearts and your minds in Christ Jesus.
[8] Finally, brothers and sisters, whatever is true, whatever is noble, whatever is right, whatever is pure, whatever is lovely, whatever is admirable— if anything is excellent or praiseworthy—think about such things.

There is no doubt that this is easier said than done. But, I think it is a good goal for us all to try and achieve. Mind control is the hardest thing for me to master. It is something we all must continue to battle and never give up on. In my first book I wrote a poem called "Let It Go". This poem was about the harmful effects of holding bitterness or guilt in your heart. You can never find peace while you hold these destructive emotions in your heart.

Keep in mind that bitterness and guilt are decisions so we do not have to be held prisoner by them. With the help of the Holy Spirit we can make a decision to not hold bitterness or guilt in our hearts. If you are feeling the effects of guilt for any reason then ask God to forgive you and he will. Afterwards move forward with your heart free from this burden. When you hold bitterness in your heart you are only hurting yourself. Bitterness causes stress and none of us need any more stress. Let it go and rid yourself of this self-inflicted stress that you don't need. You can do this and you will be happier when you do. May God grant you this peace so you can experience true joy that comes from the inside out. Amen

Quiet Time

I take a moment for some quiet time
Reading my bible line by line
Meditating on a verse that touches my heart
This is a good time for prayers to start

With so many people in my life
Praying for everyone I start with my wife
Lord bless the two men I call my boys
Let them experience a life full of joys

There are always those that are in need
Lord grant them grace as I plant this seed
They only need enough to get by
Feeling like eagles and ready to fly

Next in line I think about me
Lord help me be the best that I can be
I am focused and determined to finish the task
Lord give me strength and peace when I ask

Now is the time when I listen for the Spirit
If you have a message for me let me hear it
A word from you gives me much needed insight
My soul is free and takes to flight

This is when I dream as big as I can
My dreams are guided by the touch of his hand
Is that even possible from where I am at
God says don't worry, I'll take care of that

And so it goes when praying in the Spirit
Give him your doubt and He will clear it
I do this daily before the mountain I climb
Talking with God during my Quiet Time

I believe if you are going to have a good relationship then communication is vital. The more you communicate the stronger the relationship will be. Your relationship with God is no different. Try to look at prayer as having a talk with your close friend or mentor. A conversation takes time with a mindset of sharing and receiving. For me the best prayer is when I am isolated and not rushed. I take time to relax my body, clear my mind and calm my spirit. This is how I would describe my quiet time. Now I am ready to engage the greatest power in the universe. Prayer is the fuel that makes the engine run.

The overriding factor in prayer is faith. Pray with a sense of expectancy. Thank God for answering your prayer before it has actually been answered. **Mark 11:24 Therefore I tell you, whatever you ask for in prayer, believe that you have received it, and it will be yours.** These are the words of Jesus. Faith is what ignites action. If someone believes they are going to succeed then this acts as a catalyst for action. When facing any situation or challenge, pray for God's will to be done. Have faith that he is in control and whatever happens it will be okay.

This work desk in my basement is the best place for me to find some quiet time for prayer and to search for the guidance of the Spirit.

Let me give you an example of praying with a faith that God would take control and accomplish what he wanted to accomplished and everything would be okay. I shared this story in my first book, Feelings From The Heart, Whispers of the Spirit. I think it is worth sharing again because it is a perfect example of praying with faith that God would provide. In 2013 we had a big plan for our mission trip to Kenya. We were combining two separate teams to work together for the first part of the trip which was to be a vacation bible school. The second part of the trip each team would go their separate ways to complete their own unique mission objectives.

The vacation bible school would be attended by approximately 1200 children from five different school districts. We would meet from about 10AM until 3PM to do a variety of crafts and study several lessons we had prepared. This would give the children plenty of time to be home before dark around 6PM. We always plan the trips when the children are not in school. They have three months off during the year which are April, August and December. The itinerary was set and practically every minute of our time was scheduled. We were ready to go and excited about the trip.

Okay so here is the kicker. The week before we are scheduled to leave we find out there has been a change in Kenya. The teachers had gone on strike for a couple of weeks. Now that they are back in school the government has told them they have to make up the lost time. What this means to us is while we are in Kenya to do the vacation bible school all of the children will be in school. Oh my goodness. How in the world is that going to work? It was really difficult to picture exactly how these new pieces were going to fit together. The answer simply wasn't visible so we all began to pray.

Now let's have another little twist thrown into the mix. Two days before our plane takes off for Nairobi we see some very interesting news on the internet. There has been a fire at the Jomo Kenyatta International Airport, in Nairobi and the entire international terminal has burnt to the ground. When we check this out with Delta Airlines we are told it is not known where we will land in Kenya. It could be Mombasa or possibly Kisumu. Both are a long ways from Nairobi. Questions immediately start popping up in our minds. Where can we stay on the spur of the moment with over twenty travelers? How will we get back to Nairobi? What will the time frame be? There are a lot of questions and absolutely no answers.

It was decided to just go and see what happens. We all just continued to pray and trust God to work it all out. I will never forget the moment we were in Amsterdam for our connecting flight to Nairobi. I asked the Delta Airlines person at the check in desk where we were going to land. She said that has not been determined quite yet so we will let you know during the flight. Sure enough about five hours into our seven hour flight the captain made an announcement. Delta Airlines had been notified by officials at the Jomo Kenyatta Airport that they have completed temporary accommodations for our arrival. God had truly come up big here and a lot of our questions were answered. All of our plans were intact taking us up to the vacation bible school.

After our plane landed in the middle of the night our little adventure began. We disembarked out on the tarmac and we were directed to what looked like a huge beer tent. Everything was a little chaotic but some aspects of clearing the customs process were actually easier. The whole customs process of finger printing and interviews were reduced to give us fifty dollars apiece for your visas and proceed to pick up your luggage. Nice. We were directed back on to the tarmac where there were about four hundred suitcases sitting in the dark in the middle of nowhere. People had their cell phone lights on and checking one suitcase tag at a time trying to find the one that belonged to them. I had never thought about it much before but most people have black suitcases. We were looking for forty two suitcases in this endless sea of black suitcases in the dark of night without any lights.

This is one time it was clear that God had our backs. Since we were going to two separate mission destinations we felt it was necessary to mark all of the suitcases to make sure the right suitcases made it to the right destination. Well, we had used fluorescent green and orange duct tape to mark the suitcases. God bless duct tape! We could see our suitcases from fifty feet away. All of us simply walked up and began grabbing the marked suit cases and in no time we were on our way.

Now the next big obstacle was how are we going to conduct a vacation bible school without any students? Obviously Kenya is not America and we were asked to come into the schools to share our message. We were teaching classes answering questions and even talking about the importance of God being at the center of their lives. What a blessing this was to spend so much time with the children in a class room setting. The schools let the students out at lunch so they could come to the vacation bible school. The trip actually worked out better than we had planned. God is good all the time.

These students were part of the 1200 children that attended our vacation bible school.

This was a huge faith builder for me. I am so happy that we all decided to just go and let God provide. I have had other situations in my life that were also huge faith builders. One of those faith builders came when our oldest son was four years old. We went to my friend's house to spend the day and have a picnic. At lunch time we tried to get a camp fire started but the wood was wet. The fire would start but then fizzle out after a few minutes. I went to my truck to get some charcoal starter. I thought if we got the fire really hot maybe it would last long enough to cook some hot dogs and marsh mallows.

I was on my way back and had just cleared the corner of the house. I could not believe what I was seeing. My friend had gotten a can of gasoline mixed with oil to jump start the fire. I don't know what had happened but there was a flame several inches long coming out of the nozzle. He was in a panic. On his left stood his three young children so he stepped to his right and threw the gas can as far as he could. A large amount of gas was coming out of the can and it was igniting. This created a big fire ball in the air.

What my friend did not realize was just fifteen feet to his right was my son kneeling down on one knee. The fire ball came down and hit my son square in the face and instantly he was on fire. I was sixty yards away and began running to help my son. My friend was able to get him down on the ground and put most of the fire out. However, when I looked at my son's face I saw the damage had already been done. The skin on his cheeks and forehead was burnt and peeled back. Some spots looked like the skin was gone. His eyebrows were burnt off. His eyelashes were burnt off. When I saw this the thought went through my mind that the fire may have hit his eyes and he could be blind. Emotion welled up inside me and my heart cried out my God, my God have mercy on my son for he is just a child.

I scooped my son up and we rushed to the hospital. Immediately nurses and doctors began working on him in the emergency room. Karen and I were led to a waiting room where we stayed for what seemed like an eternity. Finally a doctor came to update us and he introduced himself as a plastic surgeon. He said our son was going to be okay and his eyes were not damaged by the flames. However, you need to prepare yourselves because your son is going to have scarring on his face. The healing process will take a long time. After the initial scabs come off you will be able to see the extent of the scarring. As soon as we got home we told our family, friends and our church what had happened and many people began to pray.

Two weeks later Karen called me at work. She was crying and said the scabs have fallen off our son's face and I needed to come home. When I arrived I went into our son's room where he was sleeping. Turning him over to see how bad the scars were on his face was a scary moment. Looking at my son's face for the first time explained why Karen was crying. His face was covered with smooth pink skin. There was not one scar anywhere. Praise God and thank you Jesus!

The doctors said it was impossible. They had seen my son's face and there should be significant scarring. The plastic surgeon told us it was simply unexplainable. However, it was not unexplainable to me. I believe with all my heart and all my soul that God heard our prayers and he healed our son. No other answer makes any sense. Experts in their field said it was unexplainable, but yet it happened.

People are amazed to think my son had once been so badly burned but today there is not a mark to be found on his face. The same Jesus that healed people in the New Testament is the same Jesus that healed my son. Thank you God.

The Gospel Truth

I was raised in a Southern Baptist Church
Finding the Spirit here was an easy search
We sang hymns like How Great Thou Art
This is when the filling of the Spirit would start

There were guitars, banjos and piano keys
When filled with the Spirit your heart was at
ease
Next came the pastor with a message to give
Reading from the bible on how we should live

You knew when the pastor was beginning to fill
His words became louder and the truth would
spill
Sometimes he was speaking directly to me
The conviction of the truth is what set me free

The people in the pews would say amen
A Deacon jumps up and shouts, say it again
The Pastor repeated what we just heard
Holding up the bible which is God's word

Tom Jones

The awesome feeling of chills running down my
spine
When filled with the Spirit I felt it every time
We all have sinned and come short of God's glory
This is the start of the Gospel Story

Then the Pastor tells us why Jesus came
The forgiveness of sins if we believe in his name
Confess with your mouth Jesus was raised from
the dead
Believe in your heart what the Pastor has said

Now is your chance as we sing another song
Up front at the alter is where you belong
Give your heart to Jesus so you can be saved
Finding the love and peace that you have craved

Just As I Am was the hymn sang for me
Never the same would I ever be
At the Prayer Baptist Church we found God's
glory
The Gospel Truth was delivered
by Pastor Jack Story

I attended the Prayer Baptist Church in the late sixties and early seventies. You know how it is when you are in your teens. You are not nearly as smart as you think you are. Quite often you straddle the fence between being the Christian you should be and being the "Wild At Heart" spirit you want to be. This is actually a critical time in your life which will determine which master you will serve.

I was lucky to have a mentor like Pastor Story. There were times in my life where I walked on the wild side but his words of wisdom and encouragement never left me. The guidance of a mentor was a key in my life to help shape me into who I am now.

Matthew 6:24
[24] No one can serve two masters. Either you will hate the one and love the other, or you will be devoted to the one and despise the other.

I loved attending church with my friends. We all sat together in the same area. I remember times when Pastor Story would look over to us and say, now I am going to talk directly to you young people sitting right over here. We would all focus on what he was about to say to us because we knew it was important. There were plenty of activities for us to be involved in. Many of us became close and grew up together. Some of those friendships are intact today after forty five years.

Back in those days we still held revivals at the church. Man I loved those meetings. Sometimes the Holy Spirit was so thick you could cut it with a knife. I could feel that Spirit working on me from time to time. I believe these encounters were what made my faith so real to me. I never forgot these moments that are now all part of my foundation I have built my life on. Once I became well grounded in my faith God would provide vision for my life. There is power in vision.

The Power of Vision

It is a blessing when we receive God's visions
His vision will help us when making decisions
They are full of insights and full of power
Leading to deeds that Satan wants to devour

But Satan's attacks are to no avail
Because the will of God is what will prevail
You are guided by faith and full of hope
Faith provides good footing on the slippery slope

There will be naysayers for there always are
They see today but what you see is afar
A clear picture of your vision is in your mind
A way to get there God will help you find

Oh there will be challenges and dues to pay
Follow the Spirit's leading the entire way
Stay on God's path he has for you
Praying for wisdom on what to do

The lives we live go by so fast
Focused on our vision we succeeded at last
Living with purpose is oh so sweet
The wonders seen on our journey are hard to
beat

There is no better feeling than changing a life
Watching these changes with Karen my wife
God called the two of us to serve as a team
Our journey has been excellent, almost a dream

Many people wonder why they are here
Working day and night to reach the next tier
Maybe their life needs a new revision
Try living your life with The Power of Vision

Vision in life covers a vast array of possibilities. God given vision is not just for ministry. He is involved in all aspects of our lives. Maybe you and your family have always lived in some type of rental property but you have a dream to someday purchase your own home. You have given so much thought to this home that you can actually see it in your mind. You have a specific style of house that you would love to live in. Maybe it is a big two story house with four bedrooms and two and half baths. The house is in the middle of a subdivision where there are young children playing everywhere. Others may picture a quaint Cape Cod style house out in the country with a big porch. It is quiet and peaceful.

Perhaps your dream is to someday be married and have a family. You see yourself as a mother caring for your children and providing not just a place to live, but also a loving home. Maybe you see yourself as a dad playing with your children while they are laughing and bonding with you in a special way.

Some people find themselves in a work situation that is not satisfying. In your heart you know there is more. Many times you have told yourself I can do better than this. You have often dreamed of how you would run things if you were the boss. When you look around at other jobs where you work you think, that job is perfect for me. Still others may live in an area where opportunities are few and far between. You would be happy to have any job that allowed you to provide enough for you and your family to just get by.

There is nothing wrong with any of these thought processes. God loves you and he has plans for you.

Jeremiah 29:11
¹¹ For I know the plans I have for you," declares the LORD, "plans to prosper you and not to harm you, plans to give you hope and a future.

There is always hope because hope comes from the inside out. When we combine hope with faith you have the ingredients to form a vision. Always commit your plans and vision to prayer to see if this is truly a God given plan for your life. One thing I want to caution everyone about. Wherever you are in life be happy and content. I have seen people miss out on so many of the good things life has to offer because they are not where they would like to be. It is the little things in life that are the most important. Maybe you don't have the job you wish you had. Your residence isn't where you pictured raising your family. Never forget that you were blessed with a family. Love them and enjoy them being thankful every day to God for giving you a family.

Each day we live is a gift to cherish. Some of you have dreamed about participating in or being in charge of some ministry. Maybe you have even dreamed of being in full time ministry.

But somehow it just has not happened. Don't give up hope. Have faith that if you want to serve then God will have you serve. Everything happens in God's timing and we have to be patient.

In my first book I talk about how I really thought being part of a big ministry was in my future. However, after seven years of waiting with no results I began to wonder. Trying several different directions but coming to a dead end time after time. I wrote a poem called "When God Seems Distant" where I shared the feelings I had once doubt had set in to my life. I wondered, God where are you? I really thought you were leading me towards a ministry but where is it? It has been seven years and nothing has happened. When I think back on it now, I see there were things happening. God was preparing me for the upcoming ministry by having me take tiny steps to improve myself.

Also, the timing was not right. Our church was not interested in Compassion International because the sponsored children were scattered all over the globe. Our church was more interested in becoming involved with a specific community. They wanted to be able to develop relationships and visit the community on a regular basis. Finally, Compassion International presented our church with a new opportunity called Church To Church. We could partner with a specific church and sponsor children that lived in the surrounding community. Now you can build a ministry. When

we were asked the lead this ministry we were
ready to say yes. I believe God had given me this
vision of being part of a big ministry and then
holding it from me for a purpose. My heart was so
ready to be involved that when this opportunity
came up to start a ministry in Kenya, I immediately
said yes. I knew it was time.

Ecclesiastes 3:1-11 There is a time for everything,
   and a season for every activity under the
heavens:
2   a time to be born and a time to die,
     a time to plant and a time to uproot,
3   a time to kill and a time to heal,
     a time to tear down and a time to build,
4   a time to weep and a time to laugh,
     a time to mourn and a time to dance,
5   a time to scatter stones and a time to gather
them,
     a time to embrace and a time to refrain from
embracing,
6   a time to search and a time to give up,
     a time to keep and a time to throw away,
7   a time to tear and a time to mend,
     a time to be silent and a time to speak,
8   a time to love and a time to hate,
     a time for war and a time for peace.
9 What do workers gain from their toil? 10 I have
seen the burden God has laid on the human
race. 11 He has made everything beautiful in its
time.

This is a picture of the original fifty children that our church sponsored. This was the beginning of our ministry that now has over five hundred children sponsored in Kenya. God has blessed this ministry in a huge way and we give him all the glory.

Home Free

Life isn't always honey and roses
Everything you try to do the Devil opposes
Things begin to change and not go your way
Sitting alone in the evening after another bad
day

The hits you take in life are hard to bear
You just need a friend or someone to care
All the emotions you have are locked inside
The freely flowing fountain in you has dried

Now there is no joy and there is no peace
You pray for all your problems to immediately
cease
Your prayers go unanswered or so it seems
You have lost all hope along with your dreams

Retreating farther and farther into your shell
You become trapped in a self-inflicted cell
Caught in a downward spiral with no escape
A once colorful life has become a barren
landscape

Tom Jones

Your stress increases and health begins to fail
Friends try to help you but to no avail
The light at the end of the tunnel is almost out
Never losing your faith in God is what it's about

Drowning in a bottle to find the answer
The effects of the bottle are as bad as cancer
Maybe you thought drugs would be your ticket
But this only takes you deeper into the thicket

Life has no meaning but God there must be
more
Your depression has tested you to the core
The light in the tunnel is out and you continue to
fall
You summon the Spirit and he hears your call

With guidance of the Spirit your life is rebuilt
Shedding your addictions along with the guilt
Again you are living being all you can be
Your faith in God is what brought you
Home Free

We all experience times in our lives where we are shaken beyond what we think we can stand. Problems come as we journey through this life and that is a fact. Everyone handles their problems differently and there isn't a one size fits all solution. The most important thing in life no matter what happens is your faith in God. God is always there even when you can't see him or feel him. Your faith is what always gives you hope. Never think that you are alone because you are not. The Spirit dwells inside you in the good times and the worst of times.

We do not always have the strength to carry on when disaster hits. But remember this, the Spirit inside of you has more power than you can imagine. We can draw on this power to help us get through anything we face. So do not be afraid when evil comes into your life. No matter how long or how dark that tunnel may seem you have to keep moving forward. When you put your faith in God the Spirit will assist you and give you strength and renewed energy. I have heard it said many times the most important thing isn't what happens to you but instead what you do when it happens. May God bless you on your journey and give you a life that is filled with purpose and peace. Amen.

Psalm 23
A psalm of David.
[1] The LORD is my shepherd, I lack nothing.
[2] He makes me lie down in green pastures,
he leads me beside quiet waters,
[3] he refreshes my soul.
He guides me along the right paths
for his name's sake.
[4] Even though I walk
through the darkest valley,[a]
I will fear no evil,
for you are with me;
your rod and your staff,
they comfort me.
[5] You prepare a table before me
in the presence of my enemies.
You anoint my head with oil;
my cup overflows.
[6] Surely your goodness and love will follow me
all the days of my life,
and I will dwell in the house of the LORD
forever.

CHAPTER TWO
MINISTRY MOMENTS

INTRODUCTION

When Karen and I agreed to lead an African ministry in Nairobi, Kenya we never realized our lives would be changed forever. We had been involved with Compassion International for years volunteering at a variety of events. Having the opportunity to be part of a three way partnership between our church, Compassion and another church in an emerging world country is truly a blessing. God's hand has been on this ministry from day one.

The ministry began with the Redeemed Gospel Church in the Kochland community of the Korogocho Slum. Korogocho is an area of less than one square mile on the northeast corner of Nairobi but has a population of nearly 300,000 people. When we became partners our church sponsored fifty children.

Now we are partnered with three more churches in the rural area in Makueni. Today nearly 500 children have been sponsored through our ministry. We give God the glory. We have always tried to follow the guidance of the Spirit.

Tom Jones

The Spirit Led

Was it by chance or was it the Spirit
It had to be God the way I see it
When you look back at how the pieces fit
You cannot deny it not even a bit

The Spirit led me to go on a mission
He gave me a nudge and then a vision
It made no sense to call on me
A missionary in Kenya it just can't be

I said yes for I thought I should
Trusting God to do all I could
Lives have been changed that's for sure
The Spirits leading was clear and pure

I've seen hearts melt when they see
Their sponsored child living in poverty
An overwhelming urge in them to fix it
But love and acceptance is the ticket

Any time you feel the move of the Spirit
It's deep in your heart with no way to clear it
The Spirit's leading is something I love
It's like receiving a message from above.

Simply not knowing what to expect
You pray constantly your fears to forget
Moving forward walking in God's will
Blessings keep coming, your heart to fill

In my first book "Feelings From The Heart, Whispers of the Spirit" I told the story of how we began in this ministry. Also, I shared how reluctant I was to say yes to going to Africa. For two weeks in my morning quiet time the thought of Africa dominated my thought. Although I tried to think about something else I simply could not clear my mind. The Holy Spirit was leading me into this ministry. Without this firm nudge I never would have become involved in this ministry. Any thought of leading an African ministry had never even remotely crossed my mind. Now this ministry is one of the highlights of my life.

God's hand has been on this ministry from the beginning. I have watched God work in the lives of team members before the mission trip as well as during the trip. I remember one trip we were struggling to recruit team members. The number we needed was seven and we were stuck on six. The deadline was Sunday. In hind sight God had started a sequence of events to secure the seventh team member.

I will tell the story from the beginning because we were blessed as well. Our neighbors had been having their woods logged. I contacted the logger to see if he would want to take some of our trees. We could definitely use some extra cash to help pay for our trip to Kenya. That year the cost of the mission trip for both of us was $5400. After a long walk and plenty of discussion the logger had determined he did not want any of our trees. I was actually depending on that money but he said our trees were just too small. When I told Karen we were both disappointed but there wasn't anything we could do.

Well not quite anything because we began to pray. We really needed the cash that year and we were also short one team member. Two more weeks went by and no prospects came forward to fill our team. The deadline to field a team was less than a week away. I was doing some yard work when unexpectedly the logger pulled into the drive way. He rolled his window down and said every time he drives by our house he sees a nice walnut tree out by the road. He asked if we could take another walk through the woods.

As soon as we stepped into the woods the logger saw things totally different. We walked the same route as before looking at the same trees. Immediately he said there is nothing wrong with that tree. He turned to his right and said those two trees look good. What really touched my heart was when he said he had no idea why he pulled into the driveway because he had already seen my trees and he knew they were too small. Well maybe he did not know why he pulled in but I did. God was answering our prayer. I was filled with anticipation and I had those familiar cold chills up my spine.

The logger went back to his truck for a tape measure and his notebook. He measured one tree after another until he was ready to work up a price. After entering all of the trees into his calculator he turned to me and said I can give you $5400 for the trees. Instantly those cold chills came back as I received confirmation that God was at work. First the logger had no idea why he came back and now he just quoted me a price that was the exact amount of the trip. Some would say it was coincidence, but I say not a chance. Thank you Lord.

Phillipians 4:19 And my God will supply every need of yours according to his riches in glory in Christ Jesus.

This is a great story but it does not end there. Karen and I kept praying for that seventh person to complete our team. We were looking at the money for the trees as a gift from God. On Saturday we had decided if someone comes to church tomorrow that is really feeling led to go but they do not have the money we were going to give them half of the tree money to pay their way. An announcement was in the bulletin to meet us in the guest reception room if you were interested in going to Kenya.

Finally at the end of the last service a woman about our age came in to speak with us about the trip. She was a widow and she said God was leading her to go on this mission. However, there was a one problem. She wasn't working and she did not have any money. I began telling her the story about how God had provided funds from the logging of trees that we were told were too small. When I told her we would give her enough of the log money to pay for her trip she began crying. Then we all began crying. She said she knew God was telling her to go but it didn't make any sense because of her lack of any available funds. She just felt led to come and check out the trip.

God had provided our seventh team member, who I will call Debbie, and the trip was a go. We began preparing the team with all of the information they needed. We covered things like passports, visas, shots, cultural training, and some advice on how to raise support for their trip. Debbie was excited to tell us her small group was going to help her with fund raising. Then she came to us with the most bizarre story about the power company. She had received a letter from the power company saying that a few years ago after her husband had passed, they mistakenly had billed her twice for her power. They had billed her and also her deceased husband. They apologized for their error and with the letter was a check for $1000.

I will never forget the moment when Debbie came to us and said does anyone going on the trip need some help raising their funds. I now have more money than I need to pay for the trip. More tears flowed as we again experienced God moving and we have not even gone on the trip yet. It seems like Karen and I would get used to this happening but we are amazed every time. The feeling is powerful and we thank God so much.

That night Karen and I were talking about Debbie and thanking God for blessing her with adequate funds. As we were talking we came to the conclusion that God just wanted us to open our hearts and be willing to give half of the tree money away. It was never in his plan for us to actually have to follow through on our offer we had made to Debbie. Also, our trip was now fully funded with the money from the trees we had sold. This blessing was a great faith builder for us. Quite often you don't realize how God is at work in your life. But when you look back at how all the pieces fit into place you can see the whole picture. It becomes clear how God's hand was guiding every step of the way.

This was our first team we took to the Korogocho Slum in Nairobi, Kenya. The main focus of the trip was to begin building relationships and to see if there was a way to fit into their vision. For us, the main idea of a short term mission trip is to form a long term relationship. Also, the team members could spend time with their children they had sponsored through Compassion International. Churches located in places like this slum exist in extreme poverty. As Americans we have a tendency to believe our main purpose is to throw money at the problems so we can fix everything.

Over decades of experience a change in philosophy has been adopted by many people and organizations going on short term mission trips. Instead of focusing only on financial poverty, the focus has evolved into a more holistic approach. People all over the world including America are poor in a variety of areas. Areas such as relationships, spirituality, happiness, or quality of life are aspects of life that even people with resources can be experiencing a form of poverty. This really hit home for me when we took our first team to the Korogocho Slum.

The team felt like we should be taking something with us to give to the Redeemed Gospel Church and the Compassion Project. We put out a notice to the church that we were in need of school supplies and sporting equipment for the children in Nairobi. The people of the church responded by donating enough supplies to fill ten suitcases. I will never forget what Pastor Muthama told me when we presented the gifts. He said thank you for all of the supplies. We need everything you brought and we will use all of it. But more important than anything you could have brought was the fact that you came back. Our staff had many conversations pondering the notion now that they have seen Korogocho will they ever come back. Your presence here is the best gift you could have brought. Welcome to the Redeemed Gospel church.

This was a pivotal moment for me. There certainly is a place to partner with churches to help finance their vision. For example when we first began talking with Pastor Muthama of the Redeemed Gospel Church he identified education as their number one priority. We were able to partner with them and Compassion International to build an educational resource center. Now the children have access to computers and a library. The children's national test scores are rising as the resource center is heavily utilized. This project has given faith, hope and a chance to all of these children.

However what we have learned is short term missions are much more than that. We have taken the holistic approach to fight many different forms of poverty. I read several books on cross cultural ministries before we began this journey. One statement that really made me think was, a lot of people living in extreme poverty are one friend away from escaping the chains of the effects of that poverty. By becoming friends the person in extreme poverty can often develop a different mindset about their life. Relationships have a much greater value than resources.

Let me give you an example of two people living in the same location with the same set of circumstances but possess two totally different views of their life. One person says I live in Korogocho where I have no resources, no value and no hope. Why did God condemn me to such a fate as this place. Another person says I live in Korogocho where even though I do not have any resources I have friends and family. We have hope because we are helping each other which makes each of us valuable to one another. Thank you God for the relationships you have given to me.

I believe there is only one poor person here. The poor person only saw their financial situation. The other person saw their life from a much more holistic viewpoint. When we are on a short term mission we are trying to change the perspective of the person that only see their life from a resources view. There is so much more to life than material things we acquire.

Matthew 6:19,20

"Do not store up for yourselves treasures on earth, where moths and vermin destroy, and where thieves break in and steal.
But store up for yourselves treasures in heaven, where moths and vermin do not destroy, and where thieves do not break in and steal.

Searching For The Spirit

Moved by the Spirit

We have three new partners in Makueni
Located three hours south of Nairobi
This is the land of the Kamba Tribe
Dusty and dry are the words to describe

The lack of rain amidst a long drought
Finding a solution is what it's about
Big tanks are set and eaves are installed
Ready to catch the rain when they are called

The tanks were installed before the rainy season
But there was no rain for some strange reason
No rain for almost a year to the day
I was stunned and sad with nothing to say

The pastor was addressing all of us
The need for rain is an absolute must
The situation is dire but no need to fear it
Because I just felt moved by the Spirit

I looked to the sky clear and blue
It was 85 degrees and I knew what to do
The Spirit has led me in a powerful way
I asked the pastor for rain could I pray

Tom Jones

I asked God for some rain if he's in the mood
Their crops need to grow so they can have some
food
Our time here was done so back to Nairobi
Lord please bring some rain for them to see

I slept well all night and in the morning
I received a text without any warning
They had gotten some showers in the night
Perhaps better times were now in sight

We took a day off mission for some recreation
It was time to see animals in God's creation
We sent up prayers with all our might
Makueni received more good rain in the night

The Spirit moved and the word was plain
Stand up and ask I will send the rain

Makueni is home to the Kamba Tribe. It is often referred to as Kamba Land. The Kamba Tribe is part of a much larger group called the Bantu People. The cradle land of the Bantu was the Niger Basin which is between the Cameroon Highlands and the Baunchi Plateau in Nigeria. A massive migration began about 3000 years ago. The Kamba was part of the migration that moved to the eastern region of Africa and eventually settled in Kenya around 1000-1300AD

There were many reasons for this migration. Cameroon became overpopulated and as a result good farmland and grazing land became scarce. Also, over thousands of years there have been areas of Africa that were moist and fertile but hit by drought. The home of the Kamba was hit by drought and widespread famine was a serious problem. There was no other choice but to move.

The Kamba made their living by farming and pastoralism. The men are excellent wood carvers and the women are known for their high quality baskets. When the Kamba arrived in Kenya they settled in the huge area which is now called Makueni. This area was fertile and was covered with expansive grass lands. However, in the late 1990s this area was hit by drought. The drought continues to this day.

Our church had partnered with five communities in Makueni and Compassion International. A series of large water tanks were installed to catch rain water from the roofs of their churches and other buildings during the rainy season. This water would help carry them through the dry part of the year.

In 2016 there was not any rain received during the rainy season in September and October. Even though the tanks were ready to go in August they had no water in them when we arrived in April of 2017. This was heartbreaking because there were not any crops grown and water had become scarce. This entire area was at a critical stage. I was told they were hoping it would rain in the next three weeks. Water is life and they desperately needed rain.

I am going to tell you what happened and you make of it what you will. We were listening to the presentation from the Kathyaka Baptist Church in Makueni. They were talking about the lack of rain and my heart became heavy. I looked up to the sky and it was blue as far as I could see. I looked back to the ground and felt the heat radiating up into my face. I closed my eyes and I felt the Holy Spirit say stand up and pray for rain. I gently interrupted and asked if I could pray for rain. The answer was absolutely yes please, pray for us to receive rain.

We returned to Nairobi to begin the second leg of our mission in the Korogocho slum. The next morning I had received a text which read we received rain showers in the night. The next night I got up in the middle of the night and checked the time on my phone. At 2:51 AM I had received another text that read Deacon Tom! We are

receiving good rain and our prayers are being
answered!! I bowed my head with tears in my eyes
and said thank you God. Thank you. Thank you.

Large water tanks are connected to eaves troughs
with pipes to collect the rain water off the roof.
The hope is there is enough rain in the rainy season
to fill the tanks. Then the water can be used to
sustain the residents during the long dry season.
Nearly thirty of these tanks were in installed in five
different communities in Makueni County.

A lot of people ask me, why go all the way to Kenya to do mission work. Well first of all I tell them this is where God called me to serve. Second I tell them I travel to the other side of the planet to watch God move in powerful ways. If you have ever experienced the move of God you know what I am talking about. If you haven't then my prayer is that you experience this feeling during your lifetime.

When we came home I was meditating on how God moved during the trip to Kenya. When I see what I know is a move of the Spirit and I am enveloped in a power that surpasses anything else I experience on this earth, it leaves me in awe and wonder. My body is electrified, my eyes are closed and my heart floats with a joy and freedom that I pray every person gets to experience at least once in their lifetime. At this moment I am one with the Spirit of God and it is a piece of heaven that warms my soul and fills me with peace that surpasses all understanding. I am truly blessed. Thank you my Lord for letting me feel your presence. Amen.

Essence of Innocence

They are the sweetest things on the earth
There is no way to put a price on their worth
I love them dearly just as they are
Children are children near or far

The children I talk about live in the slum
So many obstacles to overcome
Not enough food or clothes to wear
The world looks the other way as if not to care

Malaria, cholera and AIDS are all around
Death in every corner can be found
Some grow up without a mom or a dad
Living with whatever family that can be had

Living in a place with so little or no hope
Yet they are strong and learn to cope
I am struck with wonder by the smile on their
face
For they are happy living in this place

I open my arms and they hug me tight
I do what I do because I know it is right

They run and they play without a care
My heart is torn apart because it's not fair

Without a choice on their place of birth
The slum to the world has little worth
I look deep in their eyes as I try to nurture
They look into my eyes and see a future

Faith in the future is what they need
We provide love and hope as we plant the seed
I pray to God with all his immanence
To bless these children who are the
Essence of Innocence

The children in Kenya are the focus of our ministry. Everything we do is tied directly to the wellbeing of the children. In the Korogocho Slum life is very difficult. Children face a gauntlet of obstacles on their way to becoming adults. Malnutrition and a variety of illnesses have a huge impact on their progress. When we first came to Korogocho in 2011, we were told education is the number one concern. Most of the children do not attend school because of the cost. Two hundred dollars a year per child is monumental when the average wage is about one dollar a day.

Matthew 19:14
Jesus said, "Let the little children come to me, and do not hinder them, for the kingdom of heaven belongs to such as these."

Being partners with Compassion International is a huge benefit to the children and the community. All of the sponsored children attend school which is paid for through their sponsorship. In 2013 the addition of the educational resource center has gone a long way in helping the children compete on a more level playing field. There are still many challenges as the children become teenagers. Now the community starts to draw them in to a variety of activities which are counterproductive and often dangerous. Too many of the teens drop out of school as peer pressure overwhelms them. Drugs are a problem like anywhere else in the world. When they begin to deal drugs their lives often end quickly with twenty two years old being the average life span. Life in the slum is complex and most of the options are not healthy. That is why we try to instill a solid Christian base and do all we can to encourage them to finish school.

Tom Jones

Tears

God touches some hearts and we form a team
Traveling to a land they have never seen
Full of anticipation they are ready to go
What will they experience there is no way to
know

As we enter the Korogocho slum
They begin to wonder why did I come
Their hearts are heavy as they see the sight
They hold back tears with all their might

This place is so crowded and full of trash
The difference between us is a lack of cash
Later in the day their sponsored child they see
That big smile and warm hug is just for me

Tears flow freely at this time
I am theirs and they are mine
Spending time together a bond is formed
With tears of joy your heart is warmed

Part of our trip was in Kamba Land
To see tanks full of water was the plan

The tanks were empty and we felt the pain
Shedding more tears for the lack of rain

We began to pray day and night
I wish I was there to see the sight
I bet when the rain began to flow
Tears flowed freely their joy to show

Tears are a reflection of our hearts
Emotions overflowing is how it starts
As joy or sadness overwhelm our space
Those lovely Tears flow down our face

There is one thing for sure when you go on a mission trip. There will be plenty of things to get emotional about. You can be high as a kite one moment and lower than the ocean floor the next. The mood swings can be exhausting but this is what burns the memory of the experience in your heart and in your soul. In the evening we try to debrief as often as we can. As team members begin sharing their feelings about the day they are often overcome with emotion and the tears begin to flow. I love to see this because I know this memory will be with them for the rest of their lives.

Strong emotions even overwhelmed Jesus when he was told of the death of Lazarus.

John 11:32-35
32 When Mary reached the place where Jesus was and saw him, she fell at his feet and said, "Lord, if you had been here, my brother would not have died."
33 When Jesus saw her weeping, and the Jews who had come along with her also weeping, he was deeply moved in spirit and troubled. 34 "Where have you laid him?" he asked.
"Come and see, Lord," they replied.
35 Jesus wept.

We go on these trips with the idea that we want to be a blessing. However, it soon becomes evident that when you give you will receive. The blessings we receive are priceless and last a lifetime. When blessings from God are received your heart becomes overwhelmed and the inevitable result is a flow of tears.

Change The World

The world now, seems so strange
So called enlightenment has brought the change
Ideas of what to do span a wide range
If You Want to Change the World
Love More People

Emerging world countries need more food
Governments could help if in the mood
People are expendable is how they are viewed
If You Want to Change the World
Love More People

One big problem stems from greed and power
The situation worsens by the hour
Look far and wide it's a big world to scour
If You Want to Change the World
Love More People

Many people have turned to their religion
Some beliefs are not true, not even a smidgen
God sends a dove, like a carrier pigeon
If You Want to Change the World
Love More People

During my prayers I hear the Spirit
I believe the words have a lot of merit
Embrace this truth and never fear it
If You Want to Change the World
Love More People

Search your soul deep inside
Take the priority of self and set it aside
Ask God what to do and then decide
If You Want to Change the World
Love More People

Mathew 22:36-40 Teacher, which is the greatest commandment in the Law? Jesus replied: Love the Lord your God with all your heart and with all your soul and with all your mind. This is the first and greatest commandment. And the second is like it: Love your neighbor as yourself. All the Law and Prophets hang on these two commandments.

We live in such an incredibly complicated world. I believe the tendency is to over think and over analyze everything. When government gets involved the problems become even more complicated. Sometimes the simple answers are the best. If you want to change the world, love more people. This is not some abstract and novel notion. It is not a crazy dream that will probably be unattainable. Loving other people is something that we all can do. How we treat other people is a decision that each of us make every day.

What if we all made the decision to treat every body we contacted with love and respect. How would this change the world. Remember the bible story where the woman was going to be stoned. She had been caught in adultery and in those days the punishment could be death by stoning. But Jesus said in **John 8:7 If any one of you is without sin, let him be the first to throw a stone at her.** Once the people gave this statement some thought, they all walked away**. Then Jesus asked the woman in John 8:10 Woman, where are they? Has no one condemned you? In verse 11 the woman said, no one sir. Then neither do I condemn you, Jesus declared. Go now and leave your life of sin.**

I think we all would agree that none of us are perfect. We are human and we do and say things that are wrong. Before we judge someone else's actions what if we remembered Jesus saying, let him who is without sin throw the first stone. Maybe just like the woman's accusers in the bible story we would simply walk away. Then the next time we do something that is really offensive perhaps the person we offended would just walk away. No grudges, no tempers, and no hate.

Some people will say oh that's impossible. But why does it have to be so hard. We all have control of what we do and how we react to what others do. So what if each of us decide, I am going to make a change. What if we decide to extend grace instead of anger and hate. I believe this is not only possible it is imperative and each of us has the power within us to make a difference. If you want to change the world, love more people.

It is common for people to give us items to take with us on our mission trip to give to someone in Kenya. Sometimes the items can be a bit strange. One time one of our team members was given a new computer bag to give away as a gift. There generally is not a high demand for computer bags where we travel in Kenya. As we traveled to Makueni and the Korogocho Slum I would casually ask people if they had laptop computers. Once in a while the answer would be yes and I would ask them if they had a bag to carry it in. There simply was not a need for this gift.

In the evening while in our room Karen and I would relive the day's events thanking God for all he had done. Then we would discuss the itinerary for the next day so we would be prepared to lead. A couple of times the computer bag came up and we actually giggled wondering, what are we going to do with this computer bag. What an odd gift for someone to donate. We just kept thinking there must be a reason so we patiently held on to the bag.

Two weeks had quickly passed and it was our last day for the team to spend at the project. We had decided to take the bag to the project and give it to the project director and tell her to use it anyway she can or feel free to give the bag to someone who needs it. As we were on our way to breakfast Karen mentioned how strange it was to not see the hotel director who I will call Steve. He had been in charge of all the workers and over the last five years we had become friends. Perhaps he could use a computer bag. When we arrived at the dining room there he was for the first time greeting everyone with that big Kenyan smile.

I went over and hugged Steve and asked him how he and his family were doing. He said everyone was fine and he was feeling blessed. I asked him if he had a laptop computer. He told me his family had just gone in together and purchased him a new laptop. Then I asked him if he had a bag to carry it in. He said it is funny I would ask and he showed me his last text on his phone. He was asking his daughter how much would it cost to buy a computer bag. When his daughter had replied $18 to $25 he said there was no way he could afford such a luxury. I gave him a big smile and told him I had been looking for him for two weeks. After telling him the computer bag story I gladly gave it to him and he hugged me so hard I thought my neck would break.

We have always taught our teams that when we are in Kenya we are on mission everywhere we go. We are representing God not only in the projects but also in the hotel, the shopping center or even sightseeing. We all should be attentive to the Spirit and try to be a blessing to anyone and everyone we come in contact with. Here was the perfect example. Steve asked us to take a picture of him with his new bag. He asked us to tell the person who donated it, thank you and God bless you. He would have never purchased a bag for himself so show them the picture of him with his new bag.

God has a plan and sometimes we need to be patient and let the Spirit guide us along that path. We could have given the bag to anyone and told them use it in any way you can. But we waited because even though the gift didn't make much sense to us we felt God would not have put it on that person's heart to give the gift unless there was a reason. Steve is a person of strong character and works hard to provide for his family. What a joy it is to see someone's face when you are able to bless them in God's name.

Acts 20:35
In everything I did, I showed you that by this kind of hard work we must help the weak, remembering the words the Lord Jesus himself said: 'It is more blessed to give than to receive.'

Water Is life

We take it for granted for water it is everywhere
But many people's homes are where it is rare
We have so much we throw it away
Others search for life and they search all day

Our water is clean and perfect for drinking
Their water is stagnate and sometimes stinking
We use drinking water to water our lawn
Their search for life begins at dawn

They share their water hole with the wildlife
Which brings sickness and death with plenty of
strife
You may ask yourself honestly how can this be?
Are they not people just like me?

Governments do their business as they look the
other way
Confronted with this atrocity they have nothing
to say
Don't they know that water provides hope
Without any clean water it is difficult to cope

This is a problem we all must address
Water is life and there has to be access
Options are many with plenty to do
It can be as simple as giving a dollar or two

I have been to Kenya many a time
Thinking of them now as I write this rhyme
Our world has become a global community
Please take advantage of this opportunity

We can point our fingers for all to see
Why look to someone else when there is you and
me
Sometimes the truth can cut like a knife
There is no doubt about it Water Is Life.

As Americans we never give water a second thought. It is just something that is a given everywhere we go. There is so much fresh drinking water that we run it out on the ground to water our grass. We wash our cars and spray off the driveway. Even our pets get the best water on the planet to drink. We are partners with three churches in Makueni County, Kenya and Compassion International. More children in these communities die of dysentery than HIV, malaria and cholera all combined because of the lack of clean water to drink. To them water is not only life, it can also be death.

During the long dry season this may be the only water available for many miles. Sometimes people are left with very few choices. Dysentery is common and some children do not survive.

Imagine getting up in the morning and you are out of water. The closest water is an eight mile hike down to the bottom of the valley. You carry a five gallon pail all the way to the bottom where there is a water source. Oh by the way it is not a fresh water source. Years ago the government created a berm at the base of some mountains. During the rainy season water flows down the mountains and collects against the berm. The water source is essentially a giant mud puddle. This is your drinking water for your family. This is also where all of the animals in the area come to drink and whatever else they do after getting a drink. Now that you have filled up the five gallon pail it weighs about forty pounds. The long and steep walk back up the mountain begins. This process is repeated every other day. Fetching water isn't a choice, it is survival.

Some areas use water holes until they dry up and the search for more water begins. When water gets really scarce violence can break out. There are villages of farmers that have some goats or cows. There may only be one water source and it is barely enough to get by. Then a nomadic tribe comes by with a large group of their goats or cows. There may or may not be enough water to handle the nomads. One year while we were in Kenya the villagers of an area to east of us had killed three young men to stop them from using the water. A band of angry nomads attacked the villages while the men were away and over sixty women and children were killed with spears and machetes. Again water is life or it can be death.

Can you imagine this even happens in this day and age. As humans we can do better than this. With the technology we possess and the money in the world that is wasted on nonessential items the water problem could be solved. There are groups that are doing a great job but they can't do it all. Quite often money is the driving force. Maybe you have not been called to be a missionary or to be a great humanitarian with a mission to supply water for the emerging world countries. But I would dare to say we all know about it. These people are no different than you and me. They were just born in an area where water is so scarce it can be more valuable than gold. Their children are dying in large numbers because of the lack of clean drinking water. Will you make the decision to do something to help these people? There are a ton of good organizations that drill wells, install water collection systems or supply filters. If all of us got on line and found one of these organizations and contributed even a small amount of money. How many lives would be saved?

Fear

It is an emotion as strong as any
What is the cause, well there are many
The obvious culprit would be danger
Being gripped by fear is a game changer

Most people are afraid of the unknown
The thought of risk chills them to the bone
Rather than taking a chance that may be great
Stuck in a mediocre rut is their fate

Endless worry over a fear of rejection
Be bold step out and make the connection
Life is so short and opportunities are few
Making the best of opportunities is the thing to
do

Life is a journey full of excitement and wonder
You only get one chance so make some thunder
Take a chance and a risk, be all you can be
Will it pay off, give it a try and see

Stretch yourself as you leave the comfort zone
Believing you will reap the seeds you have sown

Feel the rush of being fully alive
Confidence that was gone you can revive

As a child of God lead with some prayer
Pursue your vision and dream big if you dare
I know you can do more than you think
Live life to the fullest taking it to the brink

We all have fear we must overcome
Live life with faith and beat fear like a drum
Success isn't measured by did you make it
It's the journey that's important and you didn't
quit it

Do not be held prisoner by your fear
With faith and action your fear you will clear

You can't see it or touch it. Fear can't be heard
or smelled. Yet it is one of the most powerful
forces affecting people in their everyday lives.
Nothing stops movement or change faster than
fear. I believe the number one cause of people not
fulfilling their dreams or taking a risk of any kind is
fear. I am not just talking about huge complicated
decisions. Even the simplest of decisions can be
tough to make once fear creeps into the mix.

For example, I know people that want to serve in some way at their local church. This decision should be simple but yet the more people think about serving fear begins to creep in. Negative thoughts and questions begin pouring into their thought process. What will be required of me? Am I qualified or will I perform adequately? What if I don't like my role I volunteered for will I be able to back out and look for something else to try? The best way to answer just about all of these questions is to just do it.

When I was first presented with the opportunity to go on a mission trip to Kenya my first response was, no I don't think so. Then for the next two weeks in my quiet time I could not stop thinking about Kenya. I remember one Saturday morning I was in the middle of my quiet time with God. Those questions started popping up. I don't know anything about mission trips. I am not sure how that mission trip would even work. They needed someone to preach in an open air meeting with the community. I have never preached before. What if I freeze up in front of all those people then what would I do. See how that fear starts creeping in. I really felt like God was nudging me to go. After a pretty good battle with myself I told God I would go just this one time.

Was it a risk to go somewhere I had never been to do some things I have never done in my life. Of course it was. But I took the risk and the reward was enormous. My life was forever changed as a result of that decision. Now my wife, Karen and I lead a mission ministry in Kenya. This ministry has been one of the best experiences of my life. If I would have given in to the fear none of it would have happened. We are partnered with Compassion International and four churches in and around Nairobi, Kenya. What a blessing it has been to watch God work in this ministry.

Make a commitment to yourself to not give in to fear when you have an opportunity to do something new. Especially when you believe the Holy Spirit is leading you in that direction. Be bold and take that chance. What you get out of this life will be in proportion to what you put in. Why not go all in on a worthwhile endeavor and see what happens. Expect there to be naysayers on the sidelines because there always are. When you make mistakes, learn from them and move on. Whatever it is you are trying to accomplish, remember it is a journey and it doesn't happen overnight. Have faith in God and pray fervently thanking God ahead of time for answering your prayer. God will not call you to service and then abandon you in the middle of it. He will be by your side every step of the way. You will feel really alive and that is going to feel great!

In Isaiah chapter 41 verses 9 and 10 God comforts Israel with these words.

Tom Jones

Isaiah 41:9,10
I took you from the ends of the earth, from its farthest corners I called you.
So do not fear, for I am with you; do not be dismayed, for I am your God. I will strengthen you and help you; I will uphold you with my righteous right hand.

Today as Christians and part of God's church this promise also applies to us. Remember that we are never alone for God is always with us and the Holy Spirit dwells within us. Thank you Lord.

Mission in Kenya

She saw an invitation at the church
Wanting more information she began her search
Stopping by our table to pick up some info
Needing questions answered before she will go

The decision is brought to God in her prayers
Finances and fear are what she shares
Feeling uneasy and unable to pay
The Spirit convicts her and she knows what to
say

I have never been on a mission before
We say don't worry we can show you everything
and more
You need a passport, visa and plenty of shots
Then we will show you how to connect the dots

Write a letter like this to everyone you know
Letting them know where you are about to go
God will provide so you don't have to worry
There is plenty of time so there is no hurry

You have been to the meetings and met the
team
Share love and be flexible has been the theme
Your little sponsored child is on your mind
On the other side of the world, what will I find

Your bags are packed as we board the bus
Strangers have become friends and that is a plus
On a plane to Frankfort for a nine hour ride
With your bible and journal by your side

Full of anticipation you land in Nairobi
The Grace House by Ya-Ya's is where we will be

The Korogocho Slum is where we will send ya
Following your heart to a Mission in Kenya

Going on a mission trip to the other side of the planet is a big decision. There are so many questions and doubts. After we announce that we are putting a team together to go on another mission trip we usually set up a table in the atrium. People will stop by and ask a lot of questions and pick up all the information we have to give them. Some people make their decision early on to not go. The reasons vary from I just can't afford that right now to I heard there were terrorists in Kenya. Still others want to build buildings or some other type of project where they can dive in and do some manual labor. Once they find out our ministry is a little different they don't grasp the concept. The main purpose of our short term mission trip is to build long term relationships.

On several of our trips we have done vacation bible schools, bible studies, taught Sunday school or preached. On this last trip in 2017 we participated in a jobs fair. We were asked to encourage the teens to stay in school or learn a trade. We have also sponsored the installation of water collection systems as well as an educational resource center. However, we do not get involved in the construction. Our role has been to finance these endeavors because the in country church does not have the available funds to complete the project.

But, there are some people that say they have decided to go to Kenya with us. You can see plenty of emotions in their eyes. The heart wants to go but the mind says you have got to kidding. The first thing we do is have a meeting to begin answering all of their questions. Next the training meetings begin. Karen and I do a lot of training to ensure everyone is ready to go on the trip. The church also requires everyone to attend a six week training class on cross cultural relationships. There is quite a bit of mandatory things each team member has to accomplish before they can go on the mission trip. They must have a passport, visa and a volley of shots that can be overwhelming at times. There is a ton of paper work to fill out. Towards the end we begin training on whatever activity we are going to be a part of.

Going on a mission trip can be an emotional roller coaster. At times you are so excited you can't stand still or stop talking about it. Others times you feel totally overwhelmed and you can even wonder, what in the world have I gotten myself in to. Then there is always someone who tells you they just saw on the internet where there was a terrorist attack in Kenya. Of course the safety of the team is our number one concern so we take these reports very serious. We speak to the American embassy in Nairobi and also depend on Compassion International to provide us with a safe and secure trip. Finally all of the preparation has

been completed and now you have landed in
Nairobi. You are so excited you think you are going
to explode.

Boots on the Ground

Sitting in the Grace House in Kenya at last
What seemed like an eternity came really fast
A Fifteen hour plane ride has given you jet lag
You feel like a Zombie as your tired eyes sag

But we hit the ground running for there is much
to do
We rearrange the suitcases and exchange some
money too
Now we pile in vans and we are off to Korogocho
Excited but unaware of what they don't know

Nairobi is large with many pleasant sights to see
Entering the slum was what got to me
The van becomes silent as we proceed
You see trash everywhere and people in need

With a heavy heart you are a bit confused
Is there no escape or this what they choose

How can anything good exist in this place
Finding out first hand as you meet face to face

When we arrive the children are everywhere
Singing songs and smiling being glad we are
there
Joy abounds with total elation
The experience is better than the anticipation

You meet your sponsored child and visit their
abode
Emotions run high and you're about to explode
Now as you hold your child in your arms
They capture your heart with their smiles and
charms

Now it is Sunday and worship begins
Singing and dancing with plenty of spins
Feeling the Spirit in the corporate prayer
Raising your hands like you just don't care

Before you know it our mission is done
You spent time with your child and man was
that fun

Late at night you lay awake in the sack
Wondering to yourself will I be back

Our days are full when we are on mission in Kenya. Every night we try to slow down and reflect on the day. Team members are often overcome with emotion and tears begin to flow. The conditions are severe in Korogocho. When you see the slum for the first time it is hard to grasp all the aspects of everyday life. The lack of infrastructure is evident by the lack of a trash collection system. This is why the trash just builds up everywhere. The houses are small and all connected together on three sides. They are made of mud walls with a tin roof. A typical house may be eight foot by fifteen foot with dirt floors. The houses are not equipped with plumbing and may only have one light bulb in the center of the sitting room. The scene is so different than anything most of us have ever seen that you wonder is there nothing but darkness in this place.

Pictures simply cannot capture all the different aspects of the Korogocho Slum.

Then you meet the people that attend the Redeemed Gospel Church. Generally we are greeted by a group of women that are singing and smiling. Quite often they will take your hand and dance with you. After the singing ends there are plenty of hugs to go around. The Pastor and his staff welcome us with some tea and fruit. As you begin to talk with the pastor and his staff you immediately discover some valuable insight. The first thing noticed is their friendly and relaxed disposition. Conversation comes easy as they have big smiles on their faces. Early on it is discovered that they are no different than you. They love Jesus and their families. Parents hope to provide a better life for their children than they had themselves growing up in the slum.

Philippians 2:5
In your relationships with one another, have the
same mindset as Christ Jesus:

Eventually you learn their priorities are much
different than ours. Relationships are probably the
most valuable thing in their lives. The community is
tightly knit together and seems like one continuous
entity. Everyone helps each other over the hard
times and celebrate together during the good
times. Another thing quickly noticed is the way
time is viewed. I have read that Americans keep
the most stringent schedule of any people on the
planet. We plan our time for each day detailing
everything we are going to do. In Kenya things will
happen whenever they happen. Kenyans are not in
a hurry and they don't stress when the schedule is
not working out well.

One thing that came as a pleasant surprise to
me was the Redeemed Gospel Church has a big
vision for their church and community. They have
plenty of ideas and plans. They simply lack the
funds to move the vision quickly forward. We look
at their vision as an old time Viking ship with oars
and a big sail. Pastor Muthama is steering the ship
as he gets his direction from God. All the people
are pulling on the oars as hard as they can to move
the vision forward but it is moving slowly. What
we want to do is be wind in the sail to move their
vision, not ours, forward at a faster pace.

At this point the question of is there nothing but darkness in this place has been answered. The Redeemed Gospel Church is like a bright beacon of love and hope to this community. There is also a tremendous amount of good things being done with and for the children in the project. There is plenty of light in this community and it is the presence of God. His presence can't be seen from the outside but once inside there is no doubt God is here.

Then the highlight of your trip arrives as you meet your sponsored child for the first time. You have read many of their letters and probably written some letters back. Many times you have looked at the pictures of your child. Maybe they are displayed on your refrigerator to see all through the day. Now when you finally hold the child in your arms it is a whole new ball game. Your relationship instantly rises to another level. Over the next couple of days the time is spent with your child in between activities. Then comes the fun day when we take our kids to a nice park and spend the day with them. What a great experience it is to see your child laughing and playing as you build that special bond. It is a magical time.

A mission trip to Korogocho would not be complete without worshipping at the Redeemed Gospel Church. This is more than worship. The service is a celebration that is full of joy and thanksgiving. There is plenty of singing and dancing while everyone is smiling and rejoicing. Corporate prayer follows with all the people in the congregation praying out loud at the same time. You can feel the presence of the Spirit so thick you could cut it with a knife. When the service is over there has been a connection with God that you will never forget. Sadly your time in Kenya comes to an end and it is time to head for home. This has been a unique and life changing experience that has touched your heart in a powerful way.

Forever Changed

Well I went on a mission to Korogocho
What I would experience I did not know
When I was there God touched my heart
Seeing my sponsored child was my favorite part

On the plane home exhausted and content
My heart is full and I'm glad I went
Thinking deeply about the things that I saw
I am filled with wonder and filled with awe

I know in my heart I am not the same
We can be so wasteful and that's a shame
I want to make a difference if I can
I rethink my life and form a plan

I look at my relationships differently now
I want them to be deeper and better somehow
I want to do something but what I'm not sure
Touched by all the things they have to endure

I possess a story now that must be told
I need to tell everyone young and old
Here in America we just don't know
What it is like to live in Korogocho

I learned so much and I have to say
There is more to life and they showed me the
way
Life is about more than the things we own
Life is about others and our relationships grown

If you feel the Spirit then answer the call
Go to Kenya to see what I saw
You hear it in my voice and see it on my face
I am Forever Changed after visiting this place

When you go on a mission trip to Kenya you
will be changed. The things that are seen and
experienced have a profound impact on your heart.
It takes about fifteen hours on a plane to make it

back home. During the ride you have plenty of time to think and you begin to replay the events in your mind. This is when reality really sinks in. The thoughts focus on your sponsored child and the life he or she lives day in and day out. Now you know the best thing you can do for your child is continue to sponsor them. Sponsorship changes their life in a very tangible way. Education is vital to their future. Health care and spiritual training are also key ingredients to the development of the child.

When you come back from the mission trip your heart is so full of emotion that it spills over on to people at home. You just have to tell someone about your experience. This is one of the goals of taking mission teams to Kenya. Hopefully the message about our mission church partner will spread to more people raising overall awareness. The increased interest quite often leads to more people making the decision to travel to Kenya. Still others are more likely to become involved in fundraisers and prayer to assist the children and community as a whole. If you ever consider going on a mission trip let me encourage you to step out in faith and take action. Your mission team will bless the in country people and you will be blessed as well. Everyone's heart will be opened to the love of Jesus.

Mark 8:17
Aware of their discussion, Jesus asked them:
"Why are you talking about having no bread? Do

**you still not see or understand? Are
your hearts hardened?**

What If
Karen and I were called to ministry together
A situation that couldn't be any better
We talk about our ministry every day
Enlightened with ideas when we pray

What if, is the beginning of our ministry
conversation
Sometimes exchanging ideas without cessation
Talking about the ministry late into the night
What if this idea is a possibility that is in our
sight

What if we purchased goods from local vendors
And sold them in America against other
contenders
We could include their picture with the display
Include the story of their life from day to day

In Korogocho we could have a medical mission
Doctors could address sickness and malnutrition
Or maybe a vision clinic to check their eyesight
If security was possible this idea sure seems right

Bus women to the Grace House from the slum
Invite them to a seminar if they would come
They could have discussions about
Proverbs 31:10
Caring for homes and making garments of linen

What if we went and stayed for thirty days
We could do so much more in different ways
I could work with Pastor Philip on evangelism explosion
Souls would be saved and hearts stirred with emotion

What if money was not a big deal
Think of what we could do and how it would feel
What if, is the vision that dreams are made of
What if is made possible from our God above

When God gives you a vision the work involved is not work at all. It is a labor of love that is welcomed and enjoyable. Karen and I feel blessed by God to be placed in a ministry together that we both love. I cannot even begin to tell you how many times we have sat in our living room talking about the ministry way late into the night. We have so many ideas that come to us after we pray and ask God for guidance. Many of our conversations begin with the words, what if.

What if we were able to construct an educational resource center in the Korogocho Slum. The center could have computers and a library with someone working with the children to teach them necessary skills to compete scholastically with more affluent areas of Nairobi. This what if has become a reality. The children's national test scores are improving as a result.

The resource center was built next to the church. It is used by so many children overflow reading rooms had to constructed.

What if a mentorship program could be set up for the teens in Korogocho. Many of the teens drop out of school because of the pressure of society and their peers. Mentors would be a valuable asset for all of these young adults. This what if has also become a reality.

Other programs have been implemented that all started with two simple words, what if. Technical training programs have begun for informal training. Now there is a training school set up to teach moms and teens the skill of cosmetology. School curriculum books have been added to the resource center so children have access to the curriculum outside of the classroom.

I am mentoring young men in the Korogocho Slum through Facebook. In Makueni water tanks have been installed to collect rain water in five separate communities. This means fewer people, mostly children, will not die from dysentery. Funds have been supplied for furniture for their new class rooms. Funds have also been supplied for the start of an educational resource center in Makindu. In Kenya about five hundred children are sponsored and experiencing hope for the first time. All of these achievements started with the words, what if and were made possible by the power of God.

No matter what your situation is never think for a second that you cannot make a difference in this world. The words what if are the beginning of a dream. Any time you have dream there is hope. Faith in this hope will be followed by a vision. A vision of how things could be or ought to be is brought about by prayer to a God that can deliver.

In Genesis we have the account of Abraham bargaining with God to save the city of Sodom. He would ask God **what if** there are some righteous people in Sodom would he not destroy Sodom. Abraham acted on his hope and faith that God would honor his request. This entire account is in Genesis 18:20-32. I believe Abraham was acting on a vision he had of the city being spared and turning from their sinful ways.

Genesis 18:20
Then the lord said, The outcry against Sodom and Gomorrah is so great and their sin so grievous
Genesis 18:21

that I will go down and see if what they have done is as bad as the outcry that has reached me. If not, I will know."
Genesis 18:32
Then he said, "May the Lord not be angry, but let me speak just once more. <u>What if</u> only ten can be found there?" He answered, "For the sake of ten, I will not destroy it."

CHAPTER THREE
CALLED TO BE A DEACON

This is My Call

What does it take to be a Deacon
Caring for people and what they are speakin
You listen and listen until you understand
Then working together to form a plan

Many come to me and they're stuck in a hole
They are trying to recapture what life stole
Out of resources there is nowhere else to go
Their life and spirits hit an all time low

I tell them they are okay and never give up
Their faith is so small it fits in a tea cup
Times get tougher as they work the plan
I say focus on Jesus and success if you can

Encouraging and praising all the way
I am proud of you man what else can I say
Keep pressing forward day by day
Right by your side is where I will stay

I see it in their eyes as confidence grows
Standing strong, as God's blessing flows
It's a great feeling seeing them on their own
The inner strength was there if only they had
known

Praying and working as hard as they can
I know it's hard but the end is at hand
Now you are victorious standing tall
God also blesses me for This is My Call

A heart for others that has no end
This is what it takes to be a Deacon

In 2012 I was approached about becoming a Deacon. After a couple of weeks of prayer and soul searching I felt the Spirit was nudging me in that direction. As a Deacon I meet with people who are going through some type of challenge. Their issue may be financial, spiritual, emotional or some type of addiction. We work together to find a strategy that will put them on a path to overcome whatever challenges they are facing.

There are several programs at the church that are very valuable when worked into the recovery plan. As a Deacon I must do an assessment of all of the factors involved with my client in order to see the whole picture. Once the picture is in focus then I act as an interface between them and the appropriate program they need. If they are facing financial issues then the best thing I can do for them is set them up with a financial advisor. The advisor will help them with a budget so they can see where their money is going. This usually cuts down on impulse spending and curbs unhealthy spending habits. One focus is to start a rainy day fund to handle the surprises that life so often throws at us.

Sometimes the root cause of their financial problems is an addiction of some kind. In this case I would connect them with Celebrate Recovery here at the church. It is a twelve step program that is confidential and very effective. You can get involved with a support group and receive valuable counseling from someone who has overcome their addiction. However, Celebrate Recovery involves more than addiction. It covers a wide range of issues like codependency, grief, depression and many others. This is a comfortable place for them to work through their issues and come out whole and strong.

Some people are suffering from emotional issues, divorce, spiritual issues, or a whole host of other things which are putting a strain on their lives. A good place to send these people is our Care Ministry. Here they can receive Christian counseling or even simply a person to listen to them and pray with them. The healing process takes time and this is a good place to begin that healing they are in need of.

As a Deacon I have seen God answer prayer and I have experienced people changing in profound ways. I have worked with many men that are alcoholics, drug addicts, or even convicted criminals that have just gotten out of prison. They have lost their jobs, their families, their health, and their self-respect. They are caught in a death spiral that seems inescapable. It has left them feeling powerless and without hope.

However, I have seen some of these men put their complete faith in Jesus Christ. As I speak with them and pray with them I begin to see a change. They have a fundamental different outlook towards themselves. They no longer feel alone in this fight. A feeling of acceptance and hope is the overriding emotion. Along with a belief they can succeed. Not only do they shake the crippling effects of alcohol and drugs but also walk away from a life of crime. They find jobs and begin to establish themselves as productive members of society. Many of these men try to help other men that are going through the same things they have overcome.

Some of these men were to the point of taking their own life. Sometimes the difference between following through and living to tell their story to others is having a friend. A friend does not judge or make excuses for past behaviors. He simply says I believe in you man and I am here by your side to the end. I am never too far out in front where they may lose sight of me. Trying to lead from behind pushing them to succeed is like pushing a rope. Walking the journey together side by side is the only way this works. You are their confidence when they have none. You instill vision when their eyes cannot see a future. You never give up and you never quit loving them or praying for them.

In time their journey peaks when the realization comes they have touched the power of darkness but arose from the ashes victorious. Praise is to our Lord and Savior Jesus Christ. When they reach this point I always remember that old hymn. Faith is the victory. Faith is the victory. Oh glorious victory that over comes the world. **I John 5:3.4 This is love for God: to obey his commands. And his commands are not burdensome, for everyone born of God overcomes the world. This is the victory that has overcome the world, even our faith.**

This is the power of Jesus Christ. I believe these men have experienced a renewing of the mind talked about in **Romans 12:2. Do not conform to the pattern of this world, but be transformed by the renewing of your mind. Then you will be able to test and approve what God's will is-his good, pleasing and perfect will.**

These men can now understand what God's will is and they begin seeking a new path. Finding a path away from addiction and destructive behavior is much more likely if you have a faith in God. You find an inner strength you never knew you possessed. By the grace of God these men have been given a second chance and now they are whole. Thank you Jesus.

Inescapable Spiral

I have seen men trapped by addiction
Drifting through life with a huge restriction
They have lost their job and their family
That's when they decide to come and see me

They are in a twelve step for their own good
They can turn it around if only they would
I talk and pray with them all I can
I can't do it for you it's up to you man

A missed appointment and still no call
I know in my heart he is about to fall
I call the halfway house to see if he's there
All bad news is what they share

He fell off the wagon there is no doubt
Thirty more days in the clinic to work it out

He calls me to ask for another chance
I lay down tough rules before he can dance

He tells me about Jesus and how much he's
prayed
He knows this game and how it is played
There is no eye contact and he can't sit still
After forty two days he has had his fill

I encourage him, hug him and tell him be strong
I pray and I hope he will prove me wrong
I go to the house but out he was thrown
They won't take him back after the second
chance is blown

He has been using and now it's gone viral
Caught in the vortex of an Inescapable Spiral

This scene plays out way too often. I believe the person knows they should stay clean. They want to stay clean but they just can't seem to get there. Their habit has cost them dearly by taking away their job, their family, their health and sometimes their self-respect. They will look right at you and say they haven't been using and they haven't touched a drop. Come on man don't try to con me. I know what high looks like and I know how it sounds. This is when he tells me, no man not me, I'm not high and I haven't been drinking. I've been clean a long time ask anybody.

Keep in mind his breathe is knocking me over and his eyes are so red they look like they could start bleeding. Why some guys are able to overcome this vicious cycle and some cannot is a mystery. As a Deacon the only thing I can do is come along side each one of these guys and do everything I can to help them succeed. But in the end it is up to them.

Decades before I was a Deacon I worked with a guy for two years that was an alcoholic and drug addict. I remember the day my boss called me in the office and told me this guy's history. He had just gone through a thirty day clinic and now he was moved to my shift in an attempt to change his habits by changing his environment. My boss said to do what I can and if it gets to be too much let him know.

When he was straight you couldn't ask for a better partner. However, when he would drink it was like Jekyll and Hyde. This well-mannered hard working and in general good guy would turn into a mean, angry and destructive guy that I didn't recognize. He would never talk about his life or history when he was straight but he really opened up when he was drunk. As strange as this sounds I sometimes looked forward to his drunken spells so I could get some insight as to what was eating him alive.

One time I watched him twist the cap off of a pint and throw it across the floor. Then ten big bubbles headed to the other end of the bottle as he began one of his drinking binges. This was the time I learned he was a door gunner on a helicopter in Viet Nam. The things he described to me brought tears to my eyes. My heart ached as I listened and I thanked God I did not have to endure this pain in my life. I would just hug him and tell him hang in there man it will be okay. You just don't know how you would respond until you have walked in someone else's shoes.

One time he called me on a Saturday morning from jail. He asked if I could bail him out. I got dressed and went down to post bail. I asked how much it would be to get his truck out of impoundment but the officer said they did not see his vehicle when he was arrested. I took him out to breakfast and then we started searching for his truck. We began at the bar across from where we worked and the trail led us to another bar. Finally by luck we found his truck parked on the side of a country road.

After two years our relationship began to take its' toll on me. I don't know if I was naive or just plain foolish but I thought I could help him kick his habits. I had done some research in books on alcoholism and one statement stuck in my mind. The author said alcoholics don't make friends, they take hostages.

I felt after two years I had to break free so I transferred to another shift. I always remembered him in my prayers. Although our relationship was rough at times there were also a lot of great times.

In a few months this guy was fired. It was only a matter of time I guess. It must have been five years later he looked me up and paid me back the money it cost for bailing him out of jail. His eyes were clear and he spoke with purpose. I asked him to tell me about his life now. He said he had put his trust in God. He had finally quit drinking and using drugs and recently he had made peace with his life. I went to an AA meeting and will never forget the group leader telling everyone, if you don't have a strong belief in God you will never kick these habits.

I told him I always believed he was going to turn his life around and I was proud of him. I hugged him again and we both shed a few tears. Another big problem I see in many of the men I have worked with is so many of them have tried to live their lives as loners. This concept makes life much more difficult. God did not mean for us to walk through life alone without any help. The whole focus of the original Christian community was for everyone to work together and help one another. Men need someone in their lives to give them a fresh perspective.

The Power of a Mentor

Life is a journey and that's for sure
There will be hardships to endure
It's not a good idea to journey alone
But we are guys and we do it on our own

Everyone needs encouragement and good advice
When you don't seek wise counsel you roll the
dice
Someone with knowledge and plenty of wisdom
A Godly man is best who knows the system

There was a man who was my Pastor
His words saved me from possible disaster
You are a leader and I know I'm right
But will it be for darkness or for light

Which way you will go is not real clear
You could go the wrong way is what I fear
I never forgot these words that he spoke
I made God a promise that I never broke

Without this mentor where would I be
Listening to his wise words was the key

Now I am older as I take his place
Helping young men to form a good base

A friend and a mentor is more than a token
A cord of three strands is not quickly broken
Find a couple guys and stick together
Helping one another through the stormy weather

You're climbing a mountain and it's a wild trip
With wisdom from your mentor you get a good
grip
So live life to the fullest as your dreams soar
And never underestimate The Power of a Mentor

I know if you are a man you were probably raised to stand on your own. A good character trait is to be determined and never quit. Doing all you can to provide for your family and possess a good work ethic. Being a responsible Godly man and trying to do the best he can to carry his own weight. These are all great attributes on which to build your life and dreams. However, the whole idea that men are supposed to be strong and not show any sign of weakness or ask for help can be a negative. There are things that happen in this life that can tear even the strongest man down. How far this man will fall is determined by what kind of safety net he has beneath him.

Think of life as if you and a couple of guys are climbing a mountain. You are tied together with a rope. If one guy loses his footing and falls the other two guys can catch him with the rope. This prevents the guy whose has had a slip up in his life from falling all the way to the bottom of the mountain. Once this guy is back on his feet he is ready to catch one of the other guys when they fall. If you are journeying in this life as a loner then what happens when you lose your footing? How far down the mountain will you fall? You need a couple of your peers to walk this Christian journey together.

Of course life is much better if you avoid the fall in the first place. This is where a good mentor is so valuable. Quite often the mentor's words make you think and that is a good thing. No one lays awake at night thinking about how they can mess up. When you have not thought all the way through your decision is when you make mistakes. Mentors have more than knowledge. It is their wisdom gained through experience that is so important.

I was lucky to have my pastor when I was in high school. We did not sit have long talks or anything like that. He just gave me little bits of wisdom that made me really think about my life. He told me one day I was going to be a leader and it would be up to me to decide what kind of a leader I would be. What was he seeing that I was not? After taking a long hard look at my actions suddenly my eyes were opened and I could see myself in a different light. That is when I prayed and made a promise to God I would be a leader to build his Kingdom. Oh I still make my share of mistakes and more. But I never gave up on myself and who God wanted me to be.

So here I am sixty three years old and living my dream. I am mentoring young men here in the US and in Kenya. Karen and I are enjoying the blessings of God in this Kenyan ministry. Lives are being changed by God both in Kenya and here in the US as a result. The more I search for the Spirit the more peace I have. I often wonder where I would have ended up if my mentor had not taken the time to breathe wisdom into my life. While you are searching for the Spirit spend some time looking for a good mentor. It will be the best decision you can make.

I Am a Deacon

A steady flow of clients come your way
They all need help and they need it today
Bad decisions or bad luck now stuck in a hole
To get them back on their feet is my goal

Some cases are easy and some are not
The root cause is not visible on the spot

Problems can be deep and are cleverly hidden
A dark and secret history has left them guilt
ridden

All through the night I feel their pain
No sleep to be had and my body is drained
Pondering over and over what can I do
No solution in sight I haven't a clue

At times like these I begin to pray
Lord lift my burden lift it today
Holy Spirit, touch their soul and heal their heart
Give them strength to make a new start

Feeling the pressure deep down in my chest
This case is serious and much worse than the rest
But God begins to work and turn things around
A feeling of peace as blessings abound

It is hard to keep from being emotionally
involved
Driven, you work tirelessly until the problem is
solved
Emotions are strong full of highs and lows
I am a Deacon and that's the way it goes

You just can't imagine the wide range of situations we run into as Deacons. Cases where people are working but something has happened that has put them in a hole. Perhaps a big car repair, doctor bills or something like that has temporarily caused a problem. Once a Deacon assists them past that financial bind they are off and running again. I may counsel with them about the necessity of building up a rainy day fund but they are able to meet their monthly bills on their own. These are the easy ones.

Other cases are more complicated and it takes a long time to get them back on their feet. Let's say they decided to buy a rental property. Suddenly the renters just stop paying their rent. They make a $50 payment here and $100 payment there but you have to make full payments on the mortgage. Money is flowing out of your bank account at an alarming rate. You are helpless. It takes several months to get them out of the house. When you check the house it has been trashed. Your estimate for repairs is $30,000. Now you are in jeopardy of losing not only the rental but your own house too. Not to mention your savings has been decimated.

These cases take a lot of time and thought. Most of the time you have to talk with all the parties involved and try to get the banks to work with you. A short term immediate action plan is needed as well as a long range plan. This is a deep hole and it is going to possibly take years to work through it.

There are divorces, addictions, bad decisions, deaths in the family, cancer or a thousand other things that come up. It can be a roller coaster ride for the clients and you feel their pain. One of the hardest things for me as a Deacon is to not get emotionally involved. There is stress and tears and tempers flaring along with every other kind of feeling that you can imagine. Then you add the fact that you may have two or three of these types of cases simultaneously it becomes a mind game to stay focused. The success stories are what keep your flame burning and your energy level high. The best call you get is when someone says hey man thanks for the help we really appreciate it but we are okay now and we can take it from here.

1 Timothy 3:8-13
In the same way, deacons are to be worthy of respect, sincere, not indulging in much wine, and not pursuing dishonest gain. They must keep hold of the deep truths of the faith with a clear conscience. They must first be tested; and then if there is nothing against them, let them serve as deacons. ...

Tom Jones

Now She Is Free

Trapped in a relationship that is abusive
Even help from someone else can seem intrusive
Living life unloved and in despair
I reach out to them because I care

Believing at first they can make it on their own
But the seeds of abuse have already been sown
Abuse can be verbal or it can be physical
A soul once flowing with life has been cut to a
trickle

She weathers the storm and decides to stay
Hoping his hate and abuse will go away
Blinded by something I really don't know
She doesn't want to stay but she just can't go

I tell her this is unhealthy and can be dangerous
You know one day he could become vicious
I pray with her honestly as often as I can
Praying to God for her to take a stand

Then one day she is beaten and kicked out
A new future for her is what it's about

All she has are the clothes on her back
It's decision time now and that's a fact

She moves in with a friend to get back on her
feet
She has bills and challenges she must meet
Slowly but surely she comes around
A new focus and hope has been found

Building her faith by praying every day
Her hard work and diligence begins to pay
Strong and independent it's time to go
Her soul has healed so life again can flow

How women get trapped I really can't say
It confuses me and hurts me to this day
My joy is exploding as God blesses me
A woman has found herself and Now She is Free

Praise God. One of the hardest calls a Deacon
gets is domestic abuse. Your heart just breaks as
you see the effects abuse has on another person.
The damage inflicted goes much deeper than the
surface. These wounds to the heart are severe and
long lasting. As the heart heals, scars are left that
can affect the person's ability to feel and to love
again. Deep inside the woman's soul she begins to

doubt herself and her worth. Unconditional love is what they need. There is nothing better than the love of Jesus Christ.

Praying with these women and encouraging them all I can is simply not enough. I try to get them to attend Christian counseling and attend a program like Celebrate Recovery. Here they can meet confidentially with other women going through the same struggles they are. The group supports each other and with good counseling they can begin to rebuild their life from the ground up or inside out. I wish I could say there is always a happy ending but unfortunately I can't. Some women never recover and they repeat past behavior and somehow manage to find one abusive relationship after another. A soul and a life wasted is heart breaking.

Relentless Pursuit

Maybe she once married or maybe not
But two small children she now has got
It's a tough life that is for sure
But one so many women have to endure

Searching For The Spirit

For a single mom the works never ends
The life of two kids on her depends
She works a job that never pays enough
There's rent and food and a ton of other stuff

Month after month the years go by
She loves her kids, the apples of her eye
She has a big heart giving all she can
Doing it all herself without the help of a man

Oh sure she needs help once in a while
Doctor bills and monthly debt begin to pile
That's how we met you see I'm her Deacon
Assistance and encouragement so her hope
does not weaken

We talk about Jesus and salvation
A Light comes on and she has a revelation
Now she has Jesus in her heart
With a renewed energy she makes a new start

She has raised two boys with commitment and
love
She did it with a little help from the Lord above
What a rewarding journey it has been
Raising two little boys in to men

Looking back she sees good fruit
All because of her Relentless Pursuit

I won't even pretend to know what a single mom goes through. But I have worked with enough single moms to give them my respect. They possess a relentless determination that has been forged by adversity and challenges. Every single mom I have worked with put their children in front of themselves. Some work a job or they are on some type of government assistance. No matter what there isn't enough money to pay all the bills and handle those unexpected expenses. As amazing as it seems generally they only need assistance every now and then. They find a way to make ends meet. It is a joy for me to see them celebrate those little victories that would seem routine to most.

One thing I have to watch out for is helping someone too much. It can be a fine line between helping and enabling. No matter who you are working with this situation can come up. The worst thing I can do for a person is make them dependent on the church for assistance. The ultimate goal is for them to be independent and self-sufficient. The red flag goes up when you are not seeing any changes in behavior. They must be following a budget, cutting out extra spending, working more hours or something that shows me they are trying to improve their situation. If this isn't happening then really the best thing I can do for them is refuse to give them assistance. Sometimes people have to be forced to help themselves.

Break The Cycle

How did you become who you are
There were many forces on you near and far
You learned the most from the examples you had
Some examples were good and some were bad

Honesty, character and a ton of integrity
Patience and kindness shown with sincerity
These are good traits for everyone to see
Live life with purpose and be all you can be

But maybe your father was a heavy drinker
You followed suit hook line and sinker
Carrying on as your relationships suffer
The results are clear and impossible to cover

Perhaps your mother's character was a bad
example
Her bad habits now you must dismantle
Following her lead seemed to be right
Now things look different having seen the light

You followed a friend that had your respect
A new direction is needed when you reflect
Your life now has become a mess
You wish for a change and to do your best

Copy bad examples and your life will splinter
You don't have to follow, be your own thinker
You can change your life by following the bible
With God's help you can Break the Cycle

Wow. Break the cycle. It sounds easy but
nothing could be farther from the truth. The
impact your role models have on you is powerful
and long lasting. When I was growing up I wanted
to be like my dad. He was large and in charge. He
only did what he wanted to do and he did not take
any nonsense from anyone. He commanded
respect from me and there were consequences
when I strayed from that thought process. He was
a hard worker and laughed a lot. When people
came to the house he always made them welcome.
He didn't attend church but I saw him reading the

bible. Sometimes he would talk about what he had read. When I was young this seemed like the way to go.

However, as we gain more knowledge and experience we begin to analyze things in our lives. Questions begin to arise that can shake our beliefs to the core. This is a critical point in our lives. We are forced to make a decision about things in our character that we picked up from one or more of our role models. Do I continue to do things that I now believe are wrong or do I break the cycle?

When you break the cycle you are admitting that your actions or beliefs are simply not appropriate. One step farther than that, you have to admit your role model whoever that person might have been was also wrong. Sometimes I believe this is so hard to do that some guys continue the behavior even though they know in their heart it is wrong.

My father was not a drinker but many of my friends' dads were. As I became an adult and even still at age 63 I continue to see guys that are trapped in this destructive behavior. I am not talking about the occasional drink. I am talking about the guys that let alcohol rule their lives. Generally relationships suffer when the head of the house is drunk over and over.

If you are reading this book and this behavior is describing what your life is like, then you have made the decision to continue this behavior. I have picked drinking because it is so prevalent in our society. But, there is an endless list of things that we have picked up from a role model that are not acceptable. Whether it is heavy drinking, drug use, verbally abusing our children or spouses, a temper, living a life without moral principles or a thousand other behaviors that define who we are. We all have to accept the truth that this behavior is a choice that we have made.

We have decided to continue the cycle that deep down in our hearts we know is wrong. I know that bad role models that have impacted our lives are a really bad break to live with. Have you been telling others or yourself that you are like you are because of these bad role models? Here is something I really want you to think about. Is it possible you are using these bad role models as an excuse to continue to not address these issues you have?   You have the power to break the cycle. You might need help from the Lord God Almighty or a close friend or even your spouse. But you can change if you choose to. Make the decision to break the cycle.

From the beginning doing what is right with a pure heart has been a struggle for mankind. When Cain brought his offering of grain it was rejected. There was nothing wrong with offering grain but it was Cain's heart that was not right. When Cain 's offering was rejected his reaction was anger. **Genesis 4:6,7 Then the Lord said to Cain, Why are you angry? Why is your face downcast? If you do what is right, will you not be accepted? But if you**

do not do what is right, sin is crouching at your door, It desires to have you, but you must master it. I know it is hard but you must be the master of your of actions. You can break the cycle. You can do it with God's help. **Philipians 4:13 I can do all this through him who gives me strength.**

Chapter Four
New Friends On My Journey

When Karen and I started this ministry we never thought about the aspect of meeting so many good people that would become our friends. Truly some of the people have impacted my life in a huge way. Their impact took on many forms. Maybe it was their prayer or the help they provided. Perhaps it was a word or a vision that resonated deep in my heart. Then again the Christian love that we shared was a bond that was special to say the least. I would like to introduce you to a few of the people that have meant so much to me.

Pastor And Friend

The time was April 2011
Six of us responded to a message from heaven
Go to Kenya to complete a special mission
You are to help the people with their vision

A Pastor from Kangundo volunteered to guide
No matter where we went he stayed by our side
There were obstacles for sure like getting stuck
on a rock
Three wheels were touching but one was not

We saw hundreds of people and checked their
sight
The Pastor assisted with all of his might
Driving us everywhere and translating too
Perfectly accomplishing all he was asked to do

Talking one evening at the Bishop's abode
The idea of me addressing a crowd became a big
load
The Pastor told me, we need to pray
Give your worry to God and there it will stay

The next day I preached filled with the Spirit
A salvation message delivered; but did they hear
it
Several people came forward and said they
believe
Now the Holy Spirit they would receive

God has brought us together that is for sure
The Christian bond between us is golden and
pure
No matter where I am you will find
Memories of you and your family are on my
mind

This poem I give to you my good friend
Remembering the journey on which we have
been
I pray the Holy Spirit over flows their cup
Whenever they hear the words of Pastor Phillip
Your brother in Christ Tom

Six of us went to Kenya to conduct a vision
clinic. The clinic was to be held in Tala but our team
stayed at the Bishop's house in Kangundo. Each
morning we loved to step outside to drink our tea

and watch the sunrise. The temperature was between 60 and 65 degrees and it was perfect shirt sleeve weather. However, Kenyans were not too excited about being outside until the temperature warmed up a bit. One morning we heard the door opening and it was the Bishop. He had on a coat, scarf and a hat. He cracked the door slightly and said you guys come in this house before you freeze to death, breakfast is almost ready. At first this seemed funny but when you live eighty miles from the equator I guess 65 degrees is quite chilly.

Every morning as we drank our tea I couldn't help but notice Pastor Phillip in the front of the house washing the car. He came over extra early and made sure everything was in order to begin our day. When we had finished breakfast it was time to leave. Pastor Phillip would always greet Karen and I with a big smile and take our camera and put it around his neck. He took pictures for us the entire trip. It was so nice to actually be in our own pictures. He drove us all over the country side.

The clinic we used was located in the mountains. One day we were taking a side trip to visit an elementary school in Tala. We were navigating our way through a washout when suddenly the vehicle stopped. When we got out we saw there was one wheel off the ground. Pastor Philip said the school is just a short ways up the road so we began walking. I took one look back as we were leaving and I saw the pastor carrying a rock the size of a watermelon to put under the wheel. Shortly after we arrived at the school we saw Pastor Phillip drive up safely.

After the mission was completed I was scheduled to deliver a sermon containing a salvation message. The meeting was going to be outside with an open invitation to anyone who wanted to attend. The night before I had told the pastor I was a little nervous because I had never preached a sermon in my life. He immediately said that is the wrong feeling and we need to find a place to pray. It was one of the most encouraging and passionate prayers I have ever heard. Amazingly I was calm and the sermon went well and Pastor Phillip interpreted for me. Nine souls raised their hands to accept Jesus and my heart was filled with joy. When I think of Pastor Philip I always see him as Pastor and Friend.

After the prayer I put my trust in God and I was filled with the Holy Spirit.

Acts 4:31
After they prayed, the place where they were meeting was shaken. And they were all filled with the Holy Spirit and spoke the word of God boldly.

Turning Point

There was a young man who cared
Stories in the form of poems he shared
His poems about life were real
Emotions in the poems you could feel

I met him in the city of Nairobi
Where he wrote a poem to show me
A story of life in Korogocho
Conflict within his heart on which way to go

The poem was called "The Unsacred Marafiki"
Marafiki means friends in Swahili
The path he was on led to the grave
They drank as a group as they rave

These friends were not friends at all
Erick needed help so on them he called
None came to his aid, don't you see
He made the right choice when he decided to
flee
I see Erick often on my Facebook
I am proud of him for the path he took
Doing good and helping others
The true meaning of being brothers

There are many paths in this world to take
Bowing to peer pressure is truly a mistake
Follow God with all your heart and mind
Peace in your heart is what you will find

I pray for Erick every day
That in God's good graces he will stay
I am pleased you reached the Turning Point
Now all you do God will anoint
Your friend and Mentor Deacon Tom

Karen and I led a team to Korogocho, Nairobi. While we were there a young man approached me with a request. My first book had been an inspiration to him and he had written a poem he wanted me to read. At that moment our team was summoned to the educational resource center for a meeting and lunch. I thanked the young man and took his poem with me. I was eating lunch after the meeting and decided to take a look at the poem. Even though there was a little broken English in the poem the story that was being told immediately impacted me. This story was a true story of a young man facing challenges in his life. He had gone with the crowd in the slum and was living their life style. Drinking often and not doing much of anything with his life.

He ran into some difficulty and looked to his so called friends for support. None of the other young men offered any assistance. He began soul searching and evaluating his life. He was at a turning point and he decided to change course. His soul connected with God and he left these "Unsacred Marifiki" behind. Anybody can follow the crowd but it takes a man of character and great inner strength to strike off on his own path that he knows in his heart is the right thing to do. This young man had battled his demons and with the help of God he overcame them.

After reading this poem I had to speak to this young man. He had written his name on the bottom of the paper. I began asking people do you know Erick. One young man found him and brought him back to see me. I told him I loved his poem and I could feel the emotions he had shared. I asked him if he considered himself a poet and he said yes. I told him in front of all the other young men that anybody can follow the crowd because that is easy. It takes a man of great courage and character to walk the path God has set for him. After shaking his hand and hugging him I told him I was proud of him. He found me on Facebook and we started a friendship.

Erick began working with children and attending chef school. He has also taken some technical classes for the trades. He turned his life around and was making the most of it. This didn't mean he was all done facing challenges. His sister recently passed away and now Erick and his mom are taking care of her five children. For now Erick's schooling is on hold. I believe in this young man and his future is in God's hands. When we became Christians God didn't promise a life without problems he simply promised us we were forgiven and had a spot in heaven.

On our last trip to Korogocho in Nairobi I was able to speak with Erick. He presented me another poem but this poem was different. It was addressed to me. I would like to share that poem with you.

JUST NEXT TIME TOM

Hallo Tom, to meet you was a pleasure
Hope we keep our friendship a treasure
I always feel secure when you are around
Together I believe we are bound.

You are more than a mentor and father to me
Magnificently through your book you spoke to me
And perfectly the information is in my mind
I bet Tom, I wasn't blind.

Yes! I agree you've got a kind heart
May your joy never be scattered apart

Love and transparency is in depth with you
Probably you will never break them through.

Leader?... yes, I won't forget that
Evidently you are really resilient
To Kenya you mobilize your friends
Since then it has been their trend.

Tom with your continued support
Your care to us is supper soft
Truly you don't even seem tired
And hope you won't get tired.

Just next time Tom
Just next time till you come
Send to your good people our greetings
This time round it was just happy endings.

This poem really touched my heart. I love this young man and I pray for him often. God keep Erick's good heart intact. Watch over him and his family. Help them provide for these five orphaned children. Lord make Erick's path clear and give him the strength to follow that path. I would ask that through Erick many lives are changed and that will be his legacy. A legacy that says he loved his God, his family and his people. Through his efforts may many lives be impacted and leave the world a

better place. Amen God bless you Erick and may
God give you peace during times of trouble.

John 16:33
**"I have told you these things, so that in me you
may have peace. In this world you will
have trouble. But take heart! I have overcome the
world."**

Pastor Muthama is the pastor of Redeemed
Gospel Church in the Korogocho Slum of Nairobi,
Kenya. He has been pastor there almost four times
longer than any previous pastor. He could have
pastored other churches in more affluent areas of
Nairobi but he chose to stay. The question is why
stay in Korogocho? Well, I believe the answer is
twofold. First, I believe he is sensitive to the
leading of the Spirit and this is where God has
called him to pastor. Second, I believe he has a
deep love and affection for the people of this
community. He has a solid and detailed vision of
what he would like to see at his church and in the
community.

I have had many conversations with Pastor
Muthama concerning his vision. The construction
of the educational resource center was just the
beginning of the changes and improvements he
would like to see. Having a primary school at the
church that would help shape the children's minds
for the future is a priority. Vocational classes are

another way to help the children secure their futures. Teaching cosmetology, massage, plumbing, electrical, brick layer or a host of other careers would be of great value.

He would love to build a church large enough to hold everyone who wants to attend. Outreach into the community has always been at the forefront of any plans for the future. The possibilities are endless but resources are not. Everything takes money so they fervently pray for God to provide.

Genesis 32:9
Then Jacob prayed, "O God of my father Abraham, God of my father Isaac, LORD, you who said to me, 'Go back to your country and your relatives, and I will make you prosper,'

Pastor Muthama went back to Korogocho and I believe he prospers because his vision for the church and community came from God.

Tom Jones

George

We had a Compassion Sunday at our church
With a ton of kids to sponsor I began my search
With two sons of my own, I was looking for a
boy
Spending time together experiencing some joy

Here is a cute little guy and he is four years old
My opportunity to change his life so I am told
He will be taught about Jesus and attend school
Included in his education is the golden rule

Plans to visit Kenya are all in place
What will be the reaction when I see his face
We head to Nairobi to visit a park
We make eye contact and I see a spark

We play soccer together and he begins to smile
Not understanding a word he says all the while
He doesn't speak English only Swalhili
Comfortable now he comes to me freely

We go to a station to get his face painted
I summoned a translator and there we waited

She asks him for an idea, tell us if you can
George turns to me and says Spider Man

It's time for lunch and man can he eat
Finishing chicken, fries and banana was quite a
feat
Wondering all the while are we connecting
Will this visit have the outcome I was expecting

Holding my name tag he says my name is Tome
I hope he remembers me when he is home
The day went so fast and it's time to leave
My eyes behold something hard to believe

At the top of the steps is my little man
He sees me coming and reaches out his hand
Others tried to help him but he made a fuss
George only wanted me to take him to the bus

This was a great moment for me when I realized
that George and I had connected on a personal level.
Very few Compassion International sponsors ever visit
their child. The experience is special and life changing.
You know all of the nuts and bolts of how sponsorship
works. The child gets their schooling paid for, with
medical checkups and treatment being part of the deal.
There is training in the physical, spiritual, economic and
social aspects of everyday life. However, you have no

idea what it is like to see your sponsored child and hold them in your arms. Relating to your child is a totally different ball game at that point.

What a blessed day that was. I don't know if you are familiar with Compassion International. They are a child advocacy organization. With this organization you contribute a monthly sum and the children are guaranteed certain amenities. Your sponsorship allows the staff of the Child Development Center to provide Bible teaching, health screening, health care and education, activities, tuition, uniforms and textbooks. The center staff will also provide meetings and educational seminars for the parents or guardians of the child. The main difference with Compassion is the projects are Christ centered and administered by the local church. Compassion International exists as an advocate for children, to release them from their spiritual, economic, social and physical poverty and enable them to become responsible and fulfilled Christian adults.

I sponsored George when he was four years old and now he is ten. I enjoy sending him letters and receiving his letters in return. It is fascinating to think I am having an impact on this child's life and his family right from my kitchen table by simply writing him letters. What a tremendous experience it is to actually visit George making eye contact and holding in my arms. This is a special gift for the both of us to form this bond.

Psalm 140:12 I know that the Lord secures justice for the poor and upholds the cause of the needy.

I visit George almost every year and he is doing well. He continues to improve in school and is developing into a fine young man. It has been fun watching him progress as well as he has. This year he is ten years old and he writes my letters in English. That is really cool to be bilingual at ten years old. I believe one day George will be a leader in his community.

Conclusion

If you have ever thought to yourself there must me more to life than what you are experiencing then there probably is. Your heart is restless and you have a desire for your life to be not only successful but also significant. You want your life to have meaning. Perhaps you need to change your focus or direction. Let me encourage and challenge you to spend much time in prayer and meditation. During your quiet time listen for the leading of the Holy Spirit. I believe if you earnestly search for the Spirit then you will find the Spirit and your life will change in positive ways.

Shift your focus from yourself and your needs to other people and their needs. Shift your focus from your will to God's will and seek the path that will give your life purpose. My prayer for you is to experience joy and peace as you journey through this gift of life. Always follow your heart as you live your life Searching For The Spirit.